Donne
and the Resources
of Kind

Donne
and the Resources
of Kind

Edited by
A. D. Cousins and Damian Grace

Madison • Teaneck
Fairleigh Dickinson University Press
London: Associated University Presses

Associated University Presses
440 Forsgate Drive
Cranbury, NJ 08512

Associated University Presses
16 Barter Street
London WC1A 2AH, England

Associated University Presses
P.O. Box 338, Port Credit
Mississauga, Ontario
Canada L5G 4L8

The paper used in this publication meets the requirements of the American National Standard for Permanence of Paper for Printed Library Materials Z39.48-1984.

Library of Congress Cataloging-in-Publication Data

Donne and the resources of kind / edited by A.D. Cousins and Damian Grace.
    p. cm.
  Includes bibliographical references and index.
  ISBN 0-8386-3901-1 (alk. paper)
    1. Donne, John, 1572–1631—Criticism and interpretation.   2. Literary form.
  I. Cousins, A. D., 1950–   II. Grace, Damian.
  PR2248 .D66   2002
  821′.3—dc21   2001033089

PRINTED IN THE UNITED STATES OF AMERICA

Contents

Donne
and the Resources
of Kind

Donne and the Resources of Kind

A. D. Cousins

Some books have focused on particular texts by Donne, or on groups of texts by him, in relation to specific genres; others have discussed Donne's writings as a whole and, in doing so, have considered matters of genre.[1] As far as I am aware, however, this is the first book to study Donne's writings in verse and prose chiefly in relation to "the resources of kind." That phrase is of course borrowed from the title of Rosalie L. Colie's learned and entertaining *The Resources of Kind: Genre-Theory in the Renaissance*; but the borrowing serves to indicate not only the book's main concern.[2] It indicates, too, that the notions of genre severally used by the contributors to this present study are historicist: various in theoretical affiliation and emphasis but nonetheless historicist rather than formalist. However there has been no attempt, in the planning of this book, to favor one mode of historicist criticism, just as there has been no attempt to discuss all Donne's texts and their multifarious relations to the kinds. The former seemed undesirable, if practicable; the latter, certainly desirable but impracticable within the scope of what can reasonably be attempted here.

In introducing the subsequent essays, I should like initially to consider a few of Donne's best-known poems, focusing on them in order to suggest some ways in which study of their relations to resources, and likewise problems, of kind may illuminate their interpretation. Then will follow discussion of how other contributors, in focusing on matters of genre, have shed new light on interpretation of the Donne canon. A useful starting point, for my purposes, is this remark in *The Formal Method in Literary Scholarship*: "The artist must learn to see reality with the eyes of the genre."[3] If particular genres offered Donne one or a group of perspectives on the world, how did he use what they made available? How, for example, did he enlarge or diminish, redirect, modify or replicate those perspectives? Moreover, how do genres interact in the Donne canon and how did his choices of genre relate to concepts of a hierarchy of genres? Finally, and in connection with the previous question, how did Donne's choices and uses of genres relate to their social functions and implications—insofar as they can now be known? In exploring those questions I shall consider mainly three poems: Elegie 19; "The Sunne Rising"; and "Batter my heart, three person'd God. . . ." Bringing those questions and those poems together, I shall suggest, may illuminate both the younger Donne's invention of genealogies for himself as a writer and a motif recurrent in his verse throughout his career as a poet. Then, as has been implied above, will follow discussion of how such questions are explored by the other contributors.[4]

DONNE AND GENRE: GENEALOGIES AND UTOPIAS

The Ovidian lineage of Elegie 19 links it to many other English texts that appeared in either the later 1580s or the 1590s; nonetheless, to reflect on the poem's generic connections is to conclude that Donne, in writing it, did not merely align himself with the emerging literary fashion for Ovid unmoralized but rather drew strategically on the resources of kind. Insofar as his poem is based on Ovid's elegies—particularly but not exclusively on Amores 1,5—it has connections with Hero and Leander and with Venus and Adonis (although, of course, they are narrative poems). Marlowe's narrator, despite the indebtedness of Hero and Leander to Musaeus, appears to be modeled on the persona of Amores, as might not be unexpected given Marlowe's close interest in that work. Moreover, Shakespeare's narrator has likenesses to both the persona of Amores and the narrator of Metamorphoses.[5] The Ovidian combination of features that Donne's persona shares with the Marlovian and Shakespearean narrators can be partly delineated as follows. He seems to be—or wants to be seen as—wise in the ways of the world, of the flesh, and of letters, too sophisticated to take social or moral convention at face value, self-assertive and self-centred, ingenious, subversive, and fond of displaying rhetorical virtuosity, at once expansively and in brief.[6] And, as will be specified presently, Donne's persona functions like the narrators in the epyllia despite an important difference from them.

The difference is, of course, that Marlowe's narrator and Shakespeare's tend to focus on male rather than on female beauty whereas Donne's persona certainly does not. In Hero and Leander, for example, the narrator focuses intimately on the flesh of Leander, having closely described the attire of Hero; in *Venus and Adonis*, the narrator repeatedly makes Venus appear grotesque or merely comic but celebrates the attractions of a feminized Adonis who, if also comic, is notionally more desirable than the goddess of love and beauty. That is to say, the narrators of the epyllia devalue the sexuality of Hero and of Venus to put forward Leander and Adonis as objects of desire for the implied male reader.[7] In Elegie 19, on the other hand, Donne's persona sets a faceless, voiceless, refigured woman on display for the implied male reader. But beyond that difference lies a similarity, one illuminated by further consideration of genre. If Leander, Adonis, and the fictive mistress are set on display for the implied male reader, so too are the narrators and persona, as well as the implied and the real authors, who display them. Marlowe and Shakespeare use the epyllion, and especially their narrators, for self-display: to display their talents in the competition for patronage. Donne uses the elegy, and of course especially his persona, to display his talents *inter pares impares*. Male self-display and competition thus link the Marlovian and Shakespearean narrators, and Donne's persona, beyond differences of sexual focus—and of genre.

Yet, in the context of male self-display and competition, it is consideration of genre that seems most to illuminate Elegie 19 and thence the Elegies as a whole. Choosing to imitate the unmoralized Ovid, Donne did not write an epyllion, although Lodge's precedent was there and so was Marlowe's. He chose to write a collection of elegies; thus, he turned from the newly fashionable Ovidian narrative just as he turned from writing a sonnet sequence. Writing elegies, he de facto announced himself as a contemporary Ovidian voice of urbane and urban desire rather than as a sly transformer of myth. However he announced something else, too. His elegies follow Ovid; more immediately, they follow Marlowe's imitation of Ovid. As Stephen Orgel has observed: "Donne's elegies are full of a sense of Marlowe's language."[8] If, by his choice of kind, Donne in effect announces to his Inns of Court and university coterie that he can speak as a contemporary, English Ovid of the *Amores*, he also implies that he can speak as the newly Marlovian poetic voice of his day. Through the arrogantly, ingeniously self-displaying persona of Elegie 19, then, the young Donne metonymically indicates a poetic genealogy for himself, a genealogy that signals transgression (if merely transgression), a refusal of only respectable poetic inheritances.[9]

The libertine persona of Elegie 19 appears elsewhere in the elegies and in several of Donne's songs and sonnets, although with varying emphases on the features that identify him; so likewise does the colonized mistress of Elegie 19. One of their more famous and interesting meetings occurs in "The Sunne Rising." There the persona celebrates his lady's richness, but his encomium suggests as well the rich resources of genre from which Donne's poem is fashioned and, thus, the scope of its innovativeness. The poem begins—insofar as the resources of kind are concerned—with evocation of the aubade; however, the very words which associate the poem with that form also imply its connection with another.[10] When Donne's persona queries the sun (lines 1–3), the reader sees at once that he addresses it as if it were a caricature of the night watchman who, in many aubades, warns the lovers of the dawn's approach or arrival. Through that caricature, therefore, Donne's persona simultaneously diminishes the sun and associates the poem itself with the aubade—but in order to reveal the lyric as an anti-aubade and utopian fiction.[11]

In "The Sunne Rising," to be sure, one encounters again male self-display and competition; moreover, although the poem's setting is a bedroom, as was the case in Elegie 19, male self-display and competition are now staged on a cosmic and national level in that domestic environment. Time is repudiated, the sun is notionally translated into a new cosmos, and James I is notionally transcended. Donne's persona casts himself rather as love's Tamburlaine than as a vengeful, Petrarchan martyr for love (cf. "Loves martyr" in "The Funerall," line 19). Nonetheless, if the high, aspiring mind of the persona does suggest his Marlovian will to absolute power, one could not say that, in evoking the aubade to deny its codes of temporal and social constraint, the persona merely forsakes it in favor of the utopian narrative: very crudely put, that a Marlovian persona rejects a medieval in favor of a Renaissance literary kind. On the contrary, one might say instead that Donne's persona fashions an anti-aubade—in this particular poem, a utopian fiction of love—not by forsaking what we now would identify as medieval but by bringing into the dramatic situation of the dawn song two motifs prominent in medieval love literature and still diversely present in the amatory writings of Donne's time.

The first motif, long established in medieval love literature and with texts such as Plato's *Symposium* in its background, is that lovers can possess a special oneness, a transcendent unity: "*Cum duo sint quos unus amor conformet in unum, / Illos unus amor non sinit esse duos*"

(When there are two whom a single love has joined, one love does not allow them to be two).[12] Well after that couplet was written, Shakespeare wrote in "The Phoenix and the Turtle":

> So they lov'd, as love in twain,
> Had the essence but in one;
> Two distincts, division none;
> Number there in love was slain.
>
> (25–28)[13]

In "The Sunne Rising" Donne's persona announces of his relationship with his lady: "She'is all States, and all Princes, I, / Nothing else is" (lines 21–22). While implying, by way of allusion to the term *princeps*, the oneness of the persona and his mistress, those lines clearly indicate as well that the colonized woman of Elegie 19 (lines 27–30) appears in "The Sunne Rising" not as one or many territorial possessions but as all territorial possessions in one. Vertical in the elegy, she is horizontal in the later lyric, an all-incorporating body to be possessed and governed. More to the point, the lines just quoted indicate also that the persona claims to see himself and his lady as a world in and unto themselves. The notion of lovers' embodying or inhabiting a private world—even an earthly paradise of love—within the everyday world variously occurs in such medieval writings as Gottfried von Strassburg's *Tristan* and Andreas Capellanus's *The Art of Courtly Love*.[14] In his Sonnets, one of Shakespeare's forms of the motif occurs in 112 where the persona tells the young man: "You are my all the world, and I must strive / To know my shames and praises from your tongue;/ None else to me, nor I to none alive. . . ."[15] Donne's persona elaborately asserts that the lovers' bedroom is a new cosmos and that all riches, splendor, majesty and power conventionally attributed to the illusive world outside are now truly to be found in the lovers themselves, who form a private world within the external, time-bound world of "Late schoole-boyes and sowre prentices," of "Court-huntsmen" and the "King" (apparently James I) who "will ride."[16] It could reasonably be suggested, I think, that to have considered the motifs just discussed is to have recognized how Donne's lyric can be at once an anti-aubade and a utopian fiction.

Bringing the motifs discussed above into the dramatic situation of the aubade, Donne's persona in "The Sunne Rising" repudiates—even explodes—its codes of temporal and social constraint. Hence, he unfolds an anti-aubade.[17] Moreover, because in deploying those motifs the persona asserts that he and his lady form an ideal microcosm supplanting the macrocosm in richness, power, and legitimacy, he fashions what can broadly be called a utopian fiction. That fiction clearly has affinities rather with medieval love lore than with, say, the *Utopia* of Donne's distant relative.[18] For all that, the punning title of More's text clarifies the form and nature of the fiction created by Donne's persona. He presents the private world of the lovers as *eutopia*, the "good place," but also as *utopia*, the "no place." Now although, according to the persona, the lovers are the "good place" and that place lies in a bedroom, their eutopian existence self-evidently lies in his assertions, which is to say that it exists solely in his tropes as a declaration of status. And the very tropes which express that declaration—*dementiens* and *audacia*—are so elaborately outrageous, so extravagantly overreaching, as simultaneously to articulate and to subvert it.[19] Consequently the tropes suggest that, because the persona's relationship with his lady apparently matters more to him than anything else in the world, it is to him as if they were indeed their own, self-contained and self-sufficient *eutopia*—even though he well knows they are not a "good place" unto themselves, bounded by but excluding and overgoing the everyday world, beyond its mutability. Through his self-consciously hyperbolic register he signals his unfailing awareness that their *eutopia* of perfected desire is necessarily *utopia*, that their embodying a "good place" within the world environing them is not, of course, as artfully feigned by him but rather exists in his tropes as a ludic, passionate declaration of status and has no other place. He self-consciously presents *topothesia* not *topographia*; he announces that he is "all princes," but seeks to be monarch of wit. There is then a further important affinity between "The Sunne Rising" and More's *Utopia*: each offers a serio-ludic image of a eutopian existence. With the persona's Marlovian will to absolute power coexists a Morean will to play.[20]

There are other utopias of love fashioned in the Songs and Sonnets; not many, I think, and by no means all of them imaging love as an exercise in colonization and in autocracy. "The Anniversarie" and "The good-morrow," for example, allude to those political categories yet deny them as they appear in Elegie 19 or in "The Sunne Rising." But Donne wrote dystopian fictions, too.[21] Some of those are in his Satires, as might be expected, and others are in the Elegies. Some momentarily, even fleetingly, occur in his religious verse: the self, no longer imaged as or as part of "the good place," is represented in terms of virtually irremediable political discord, as a corrupted community, as a polluted microcosm, and thus in terms of the need for amendment.[22] "I am a little world made cunningly" offers one antithesis to the utopian fictions of "The Sunne Rising," "The Anniversarie," "The good-morrow" and other of the Songs and Sonnets. A more startling contrast can be seen in "Batter my heart, three-person'd God. . . ."[23]

Viewing the poem as, at least in part, a dystopian fiction helps rather than hinders viewing it as a meditation. Attempts to associate it exclusively with the Ignatian or a Protestant model of meditation have been inconclusive; even so, whatever model, if any, Donne used with the architecture of the sonnet in order to shape the poem, his persona nonetheless sets before the reader a meditation on his need for yet further softening of heart, for mortification and for sanctification.[24] In meditating on the wants of his soul, the persona fashions images of physical, political, and sexual violence. The central image, that of the "usurpt towne," pictures his spirituality in terms of unresolved political discord and of political weakness or betrayal: the microcosm of the self resembles a misruled and dysfunctional body politic, a dystopia (lines 5–8). Moreover, the implicit contrast in those lines between their image of a microcosmic dystopia and images of microcosmic utopias in some of the Songs and Sonnets is heightened in the poem's last six lines.

There, too, problems of genre and interpretation increase. From Carew's elegy on Donne we may reasonably guess that the image of sexual violence which ends the poem struck some of Donne's contemporaries forcibly, as it may now strike us.[25] True, one sees at once that Donne's ostentatious indecorum in having the persona of a religious poem request rape by God is carefully judged. His persona speaks, after all, as if in extremities, as if believing himself so sin-bound to Satan that only an exceptional act—a holy lawlessness—can rescue him. Thus Donne's persona decorously pleads beyond decorum that God's justice be transcended by His mercy. To see the persona manipulating decorum in such a way, however, indicates the appropriateness of his speaking indecorously at the poem's end but does not clarify why he chooses in particular to close his meditation with a request for rape. And just as that request is not clarified by reference to a broadly theological justification of decorum overgone—its being a general principle of decorum in the religious lyric, as in other religious genres, that to tell of the divine involves transcending mundane criteria of appropriateness—neither is it clarified by a more specifically theological reference, namely, to conventions of erotic spirituality. In terms of that spirituality, expressed often in meditative verse, the persona's request for rape could be interpreted as a request for his female soul to be seized by and united to God, thereby ultimately making possible the Spiritual Marriage.[26] Thus in the last line of the poem could be seen a fiction of male/female relations (the speaker's to his soul) at once dystopian when contrasted with the microcosmic utopian fictions of "The Sunne Rising," among various of the Songs and Sonnets, and looking beyond such utopianism to glorification, to fulfilment of the *ordo salutis*. Donne's Calvinism could therefore be viewed as setting in perspective at that moment of the poem, aptly and doubly in microcosm, the interplay between utopianism and dystopianism in his verse—which of course it does in any case. Yet to read the end of "Batter my heart . . ." even in terms so relevant to the religious lyric in general and to meditative writing in particular does not seem to clarify sufficiently its violent, incongruous, paradoxical sexuality.[27] Perhaps the close of the poem offers an interpretative problem beyond the domain of literary genre.[28]

Be that as it may, one would not want to suggest in any case that considerations of genre illuminate all difficulties of interpretation, whether in Donne's writings or in those by anyone else. Studying Donne's texts with regard to genre can illuminate, nonetheless, many of their different aspects, as it is hoped the discussion above has indicated. By way of example, one could mention their intertextual and discursive relations, their interactions with the social environments within which they were fashioned, their strategies of rhetoric and of authorial self-representation. In particular this discussion has sought to suggest that, through attention to questions of genre, one can discern within Donne's verse the coexistence and implicit interaction of Ovidian/Marlovian with medieval/Morean elements, and also the Calvinist refiguring of those latter elements. Donne's command of genre was, as his elegists emphasized, both wide and innovative; we modern readers are still discovering how wide and how innovative it was.

DONNE AND GENRE: EXPLORATIONS IN THE DONNE CANON

Since 1950 much of the commentary on Donne's uses of genre seems to have continued along a path smoothed by C. S. Lewis and by John Buxton.[29] Until fairly recently, that is to say, Donne's flouting the conventions of the kinds appears to have been given most attention. Nonetheless, over the last couple of decades other ways in which Donne used genre have also been emphasized. Two of the most important have been those evoked in the opening of this essay: genre as offering a perspective, or cluster of perspectives, on the world; genre as the expression of ideology and hence of conflicting worldviews. It would seem true to say that, more than anyone else, Mikhail Bakhtin contributed to the theoretical framework for each—and each has become widely established in recent historicist criticisms. A third way has also been much emphasized, however: the relations between genre and gender. That way is, of course, variously indebted to feminist critical theories and has become familiar in feminist practices of historicism.[30] The subsequent essays in this book, while necessarily concerned with issues of decorum within the kinds (since, in his verse, Donne himself so frequently alludes to such issues), are likewise concerned with those ways of examining how Donne used the resources of kind.

In the following essays, Donne's dealings with "the criterion of decorum," as Rosemond Tuve called it, are illuminated afresh. Earl Miner, for example, innovatively combines truth and decorum as categories through which to discriminate among Donne's practices in different kinds of poetry and, moreover, through which to discriminate his practices in them from those by various poets of his times. Relating the two categories to others that have guided inquiry thus far into Donne's writings and into works by his contemporaries, Miner proceeds by way of a widely ranging discussion to demonstrate the freshness of their pairing and their powers in combination to discriminate. Thus, he writes of "The Anagram":

> One way of describing what goes on here is to point to the way in which the truth obtainable from a Roman love elegy ("love thy *Flavia*") shatters the decorum of the Renaissance blazon that itemized in partitive fashion a woman's beauties. But the repetition of iconoclastic truth may become conventional, and Donne sometimes is found replacing one decorum by another.

The last statement has particular resonance when contextualized by the remark that, in Donne's unstable and uncertain times, "the decorous was almost another truth." Proceeding to consider the decorum of the Satires, for "exposing truth still requires a decorum," Miner argues that the danger involved in Donne's political invective could be deflected by an appeal to the decorum of satire itself but that, nonetheless, Donne habitually "violates old decorums to reveal new truths." Against such violations he deftly contrasts Donne's reverent, elaborate play with decorum in a letter to Lucy, Countess of Bedford. Coming to "the criterion of decorum" from a different but not unrelated angle, Liam Semler observes that "There is, in general, a retreat from the indecorously disturbing (though not always its complete abandonment) and a motion towards, particularly in the shorter epistles, a sheer embodiment of grace and style (*maniera*)." And Neil Keeble writes:

> Declining the lyrical mode advertised by their heading, the lyrics of the "Songs and Sonnets" are characterized instead by generic resistance and subversion; their relationship to songs and sonnets is ironic and parodic. With neither his texts, nor his readers, nor the women whom he ostensibly addresses does Donne establish the relationship expected of a sixteenth-century lyricist. He never presents himself as a lutenist in the manner of Wyatt (or even Herbert in "Easter"), nor as a harpist like Drayton, nor as a musician lover like Campion.

Heather Dubrow, too, focuses on decorum. She begins her essay by suggesting that the Elegies linked with the ugly beauty tradition "are in some respects catalogues of the characteristics of [that] tradition, even though the third poem deviates significantly from it in not actually praising its unappetizing heroine." On the other hand, Dubrow's essay finely attends to matters of genre and gender. When discussing "The Comparison," and illustrating Donne's status as a "resident alien" in the terrain of Petrarchism, she shows that the poem "twists Petrarchan tropes" and strategically deploys misogyny, for behind the poem's elaborate display of contrasting females she identifies male rivalry. Male self-display by way of ostensible display of the female is what Marea Mitchell analyzes, however, in her study of the *Anniversaries*. She argues that the epideictic rhetoric of Donne's poems on Elizabeth Drury can be located in a "tradition, well marked and criticized by feminism, in which the female body and character are both completely insignificant and vitally important." Further, as Mitchell proceeds to demonstrate: "By the end of *The First Anniversary* the speaker has negotiated for himself a position of authority and stands triumphant beside the slab where poetry sits in place of Drury's body."

No less illuminatingly explored are the ways in which Donne played with genres' perspectives on the world and uses genre to present or imply conflicting worldviews. As regards the former, Liam Semler demonstrates how, in a "neo-Ovidian genre"—the elegy—Donne "toned down or removed" ["disruptive and confronting aspects of scepticism"] so that "what remains is a series of poems designed largely, many purely, as effortless and novel displays of art." With respect to the latter, Earl Miner considers how Donne uses the lyric to stage conflicts between private good and the commonweal. Frank Brownlow, in his account of *La Corona* and of the Holy Sonnets, sees those poems as using religious perspectives on the world in order to represent and, in varying modes, promote the self. Of *La Corona* he writes:"[T]he rewards of reading the poem are more aesthetic than religious; it is meant to arouse delight and admiration among well-educated readers who would appreciate the range of its material . . . and admire its author's unsectarian willingness to refrain from drawing hard conclusions or pressing unfashionable enthusiasms." By way of complement and contrast, Eugene Hill closely considers Donne's sermon on *Acts* 28.6 of January 25 1629, to suggest how Donne could both restate and query the notion of the divine right of kings. Hill shows that, using an intricate pattern of allusions, Donne takes on "the intense monitory tones of a prophet, warning his King that excesses, such as self-deification, inevitably bring on their contraries." In Damian Grace's conclusion to this volume, which looks at some of the more prominent, recent studies in Donne and genre, particular attention is given to accounts of the link between genre and social power.

NOTES

1. See, for example, Kate Gartner Frost, *Holy Delight: Typology, Numerology, and Autobiography in Donne's* Devotions Upon Emergent Occasions (Princeton: Princeton University Press, 1990) and Arthur F. Marotti, *John Donne, Coterie Poet* (Madison: University of Wisconsin Press, 1986).

2. Rosalie L. Colie, *The Resources of Kind: Genre-Theory in the Renaissance*, ed. Barbara K. Lewalski (Berkeley, Los Angeles, London: University of California Press, 1973). In relation to Colie's study see especially Barbara K. Lewalski, ed., *Renaissance Genres: Essays on Theory, History, and Interpretation* (Cambridge, Mass., and London: Harvard University Press, 1986).

3. See M. M. Bakhtin [?]/ P. N. Medvedev, *The Formal Method in Literary Scholarship: A Critical Introduction to Sociological Poetics*, trans. Albert J. Wehrle (1978; rpt. Cambridge: Harvard University Press, 1985), 134—cf. 3–23. See also M. M. Bakhtin,

Problems of Dostoevsky's Poetics, ed. and trans. Caryl Emerson (Manchester: Manchester University Press, 1984), 157 and 271. While Bakhtin's writings seem to me to offer the most rich and lively arguments about how genres function in Western society, my understanding of particular genres in Renaissance England has been enriched by the works of scholars such as Rosemond Tuve, Rosalie L. Colie, Louis L. Martz, Earl Miner, Barbara K. Lewalski, Arthur F. Kinney, Heather Dubrow, Lawrence Manley, Linda Woodbridge, and Patrick Cheney. The discussions that have interested me most with regard to what actually constitutes a genre have been those by Austin Warren and Rene Wellek, *Theory of Literature* (1949; rpt. London: Jonathan Cape, 1955), 235–47, Alastair Fowler, *Kinds of Literature: An Introduction to the Theory of Genres and Modes* (Oxford: Clarendon, 1982), 1–53; Adena Rosmarin, *The Power of Genre* (Minneapolis: University of Minnesota Press, 1985), 3–51; Tony Bennett, *Outside Literature* (London and New York: Routledge, 1990), 78–114; John Snyder, *Prospects of Power: Tragedy, Satire, the Essay, and the Theory of Genre* (Lexington: University Press of Kentucky, 1991), 1–23. Fowler's use of the "family resemblance" trope seems still to offer the most useful way of working out what a genre includes and what it does not, despite the difficulties obviously evoked by the trope itself.

4. Reference to Donne's poems is from *The Complete English Poems*, ed. C. A. Patrides (London and Melbourne: Dent, 1985).

5. Although not a narrative poem, Donne's elegy derives in part from the narrative unfolded in *Amores* 1,5 (as has been mentioned above); *Venus and Adonis* derives partly from episodes in the *Metamorphoses*. For a more extended version of the argument here, one on which I am both drawing and elaborating, see my "Towards a Reconsideration of Shakespeare's Adonis: Rhetoric, Narcissus, and the Male Gaze," *Studia Neophilologica* 68 (1996): 195–204, especially at 200–203.

6. See, for example, *Hero and Leander* 1.5–90 (the *blazons* of the main figures in the narrative) as regards the self-assertiveness, the self-centredness, the carnal and literary sophistication paraded by Marlowe's persona—and his displaying rhetorical virtuosity. Moreover, in connection with the latter, see 2.85–86, 139–40, 287–88, and so on for examples of the persona's epigramatic wit. Likewise, in *Venus and Adonis*, see the manner in which the narrator devalues the sexual attractiveness of Venus and sets up Adonis as the notional object of desire for the implied male reader, chiefly in lines 5–6, 29–35, 463–68, 1057–62; cf. lines 63–68, 73–84, 241–52, 349–54, and so on. Reference to Marlowe's verse is from *The Complete Poems and Translations*, ed. Stephen Orgel (Harmondsworth: Penguin, 1971). Reference to *Venus and Adonis* is from *The Poems*, ed. F. T. Prince (1960; rpt. London: Methuen, 1961). For ready examples of those Ovidian features in the persona of *Amores* one could cite: 1.1.1–4; 1.2.39–48; 1.3.19–26; 1.4.59–70; 1.5 *passim*. Reference to *Amores* is from *Heroides and Amores*, ed. and trans. Grant Showerman, *Loeb Classical Library* (1921; rpt. Cambridge: Harvard University Press/Heinemann, 1947). There is a stimulating discussion of continuities between Ovid's earlier poetry and his *Metamorphoses*, especially as regards modes of narration, in G. Karl Galinsky, *Ovid's* Metamorphoses: *An Introduction to the Basic Aspects* (Berkeley and Los Angeles: University of California Press, 1975), 25–42. See also William Keach, *Elizabethan Erotic Narratives: Irony and Pathos in the Ovidian Poetry of Shakespeare, Marlowe, and Their Contemporaries* (Hassocks: Harvester, 1977), 3–35.

7. See my "Shakespeare's Adonis," 198–201.

8. See Orgel's edition of Marlowe's poems, 233.

9. Presumably for reasons of class, along with whatever else, Donne chose not to

speak via the stage with (or without) a Marlovian poetic voice. He demonstrates his dramatic skills, of course, through the virtuoso fashioning of monologues. I am indebted to Patrick Cheney for making me consider this point. Donne could associate himself, of course, with poetic genealogies that exceed the boundaries of mere transgression: clearly, he does so through the speakers in some of his satires and in some of his religious verse. For other views of the Elegies, see especially Terry G. Sherwood, *Fulfilling the Circle: A Study of John Donne's Thought* (Toronto: University of Toronto Press, 1984), 72–74; Arthur F. Marotti, *John Donne*, 44–66; Achsah Guibbory, "John Donne," in *The Cambridge Companion to English Poetry: Donne to Marvell*, ed. Thomas N. Corns (Cambridge: Cambridge University Press, 1993), 123–47, at 132–34. On construction of poetic genealogies in Donne's time, see Richard Helgerson, *Self-Crowned Laureates: Spenser Jonson Milton and the Literary System* (Berkeley, Los Angeles, London: University of California Press, 1983); P. Cheney, *Marlowe's Counterfeit Profession Ovid, Spenser, Counter-Nationhood* (Toronto: University of Toronto Press, 1997). For an account of Donne's life at the time of his writing the Elegies, see R. C. Bald, *John Donne: A Life* (Oxford: Clarendon, 1970), 53–79.

10. For an account of problems in defining the aubade, see James J. Wilhelm, *The Cruelest Month: Spring, Nature, and Love in Classical and Medieval Lyrics* (New Haven: Yale University Press, 1965), 193–202. See also Peter Dronke, *The Medieval Lyric*, 2nd ed. (London: Hutchinson, 1978), 167–85.

11. The poem's beginning with comic evocation of the aubade does not mean that it *must* unfold as an anti-aubade: for example, the persona could begin with complaint to and ridicule of the sun and then preceed, nonetheless, to accept the demands that the sun's rising imposes on him and on his lady. My point is, of course, that the persona begins with comic evocation of the aubade then proceeds to unfold an anti-aubade, having chosen (as it were) that particular option. For a different view of the poem's relations to the aubade (and with a different notion of the utopian) see C. Belsey *Desire Love Stories in Western Culture* (Oxford: Blackwell, 1994), 140-43.

12. From an anonymous poet quoted and translated by Peter Dronke in his *Medieval Latin and the Rise of the European Love-Lyric*, 2 vols. (Oxford: Clarendon Press, 1966), 2:468. See also Irving Singer, *The Nature of Love*, 3 vols. (Chicago and London: University of Chicago Press, 1984), vol. 2, *Courtly and Romantic*, 31–33.

13. Reference is to Prince's edition of the poems. Cf. "The Canonization," lines 23–27.

14. Reference to *Tristan* is from the translation by A. T. Hatto, rev. ed. (1960; rpt. London: Penguin, 1967), 26, 261–68. For a discussion of "The Cave of Lovers" as a private, paradisal world of love, see Singer, *The Nature of Love*, 105–7. On the motif of lovers' unique oneness as evoked in *The Art of Courtly Love*, see the translation by John J. Parry (1941; rpt. New York and London: Norton, 1969), 2.4.156; that aside, for Andreas's form of the notion that lovers can embody or inhabit a private, even paradisal, world see 1, fifth dialogue, 78–80. In relation to the latter, see Richard de Fournival, "Advice on Love," in *The Comedy of Eros: Medieval French Guides to the Art of Love*, trans. Norman R. Shapiro, with notes and commentary by James B. Wadsworth (Urbana, Chicago, London: University of Illinois Press, 1971), 123.

15. See *The Sonnets and A Lover's Complaint*, ed. John Kerrigan (London: Penguin, 1986), 112, lines 5–7.

16. See respectively lines 27–30, 14–26, 6–7.

17. The persona may knowingly or otherwise use the medieval motifs, reject the aubade's codes of temporal and social constraint, and fashion an anti-aubade. It

seems likely to me that he does so knowingly—literary play appears to be part of his ludic fiction-making—but what matters most is that he does indeed do the things mentioned above; how knowingly he does them is secondary and can be guessed at but not demonstrated. The question also arises, for example, of whether the persona knows (as it were) that he is playing with the *multum in parvo* topos: he presents a version often used in Donne's poems, especially his utopian fictions of love, namely, *non multum sed omnia in parvo*. An obvious contrast to "The Sunne Rising" as an anti-aubade is "Breake of day."

18. The utopia of love announced in "The Sunne Rising" seems in fact not able to be associated with any of the forms of utopian narrative catalogued by J. C. Davis in his *Utopia and the Ideal Society: A Study of English Utopian Writing 1516–1700* (1981; rpt. Cambridge: Cambridge University Press, 1983), 12–40.

19. It could hardly be suggested, for example, that the persona actually believes himself and his lady to have conquered time. He may be indicating that love is not time's fool, and that to him and to his lady time is an irrelevance, but he is not announcing his belief that he and his lady have literally achieved the conquest of time. Cf. Rosemond Tuve on *dementiens* in her *Elizabethan and Metaphysical Imagery: Renaissance Poetic and Twentieth-Century Critics* (Chicago: University of Chicago Press, 1947), 317–18. The most immediately relevant remark occurs on p. 318: "Ordinary hyperbole exaggerates 'that rather you may conceive the unspeakableness than the untruth' of what is being related, as Hoskins says. . . ."

20. Cf. Stephen Greenblatt, "Marlowe and the Will to Absolute Play," in his *Renaissance Self-Fashioning from More to Shakespeare* (1980; rpt. Chicago: University of Chicago Press, 1984), 193–221. See also A. D. Cousins and Damian Grace, eds., *More's Utopia and the Utopian Inheritance* (Lanham, MD, New York, London: University Press of America, 1995), introduction, x–xi.

21. On seventeenth-century dystopian fictions, see James Holstun, *A Rational Millennium: Puritan Utopias of Seventeenth-Century England and America* (New York and Oxford: Oxford University Press, 1987), 11, 106, 267–75, 305–6. See also Frank E. Manuel, ed., *Utopias and Utopian Thought* (1965; rpt. Trowbridge: Souvenir, 1973), 9 and 71.

22. I am not suggesting that Donne's dystopian fictions can be found only among those poems. It may be that the dystopianism in the religious verse is a deliberate repudiation of utopianism in the secular love verse, but of course that cannot be known. At the end of "To His Coy Mistress," Marvell's libertine persona creates a utopian fiction of love that appears rather to be dystopian and that may be designed as an antithesis to the utopian visions of "The Sunne Rising," "The Anniversarie," "The good-morrow" and some other lyrics from the Songs and Sonnets. See lines 41–44 of Marvell's poem in *The Complete Poems*, ed. Elizabeth Story Donno (1972; rpt. London: Allen Lane, 1974).

23. For a brief introduction to the extensive and vigorous debates about the poem, see the articles brought together by Arthur L. Clements in his text *John Donne's Poetry*, 2nd ed. (1966; rpt. New York: Norton, 1992), 325–49. See also Barbara Kiefer Lewalski, *Protestant Poetics and the Seventeenth-Century Religious Lyric* (Princeton: Princeton University Press, 1979), 202–3, 271–272; Sherwood, *Fulfilling the Circle*, 151–52; Marotti, *John Donne*, 259–60; Anthony Lowe, *The Reinvention of Love: Poetry, Politics and Culture from Sidney to Milton* (Cambridge: Cambridge University Press, 1993), 79–81; Peter Iver Kaufman, *Prayer, Despair, and Drama: Elizabethan Introspection* (Urbana and Chicago: University of Illinois Press, 1996), 154–55.

24. It is unlikely that no model of religious meditation underlies the poem; on the other hand, Donne may indeed have imitated no specific model. That aside, a text immediately relevant to Donne's poem appears to be Calvin's *Institutes*, 3.3.18 (cf. 3.3.7–17). Reference to the *Institutes* is from the edition by John T. McNeill translated by Ford Lewis Battles, 2 vols (Philadelphia: Westminster, 1960). It seems to me that Calvin's account of repentance in the *ordo salutis*, as set out in those sections of the *Institutes*, illuminates the representation of spiritual experience in "Batter my heart. . . ." Thus, Calvin's account of repentance, as unfolded in *Institutes* 3.3.7–18, contextualizes my use of the terms "softening of heart" (that is, mollification), "mortification," and "sanctification."

25. It does not necessarily strike us either to the same degrees or for the same reasons as it putatively struck some of Donne's contemporaries and immediate successors. Reference to Carew's elegy, line 17, is from Patrides' edition of Donne.

26. The soul is conventionally gendered as female in English Renaissance religious verse.

27. Other famous examples of erotic spirituality in seventeenth-century English religious verse occur in Crashaw's hymn to St. Teresa and *The Weeper*—and there, too, that spirituality generates difficulties of interpretation. See Austin Warren, *Richard Crashaw: A Study in Baroque Sensibility* (London: Faber, 1939), 126–58; Louis L. Martz, *The Wit of Love: Donne, Carew, Crashaw, Marvell* (Notre Dame and London: University of Notre Dame Press, 1969), 131–35; A. D. Cousins *The Catholic Religious Poets from Southwell to Crashaw: A Critical History* (London: Sheed and Ward, 1991), 159–74; Low, *The Reinvention of Love*, 125–31.

28. It may rather be related to the curious strand of blasphemy that runs through the Elegies, the Songs and Sonnets, and some of the other verse. There is in Donne's verse, too, what might be called a strand of libertine devotion—of irreverent, ludic devotional writing. F. W. Brownlow makes a related point in his discussion, below, of the Holy Sonnets.

29. C. S. Lewis, *English Literature in the Sixteenth Century Excluding Drama* (Oxford: Clarendon Press, 1954), especially at pages 538–541. John Buxton, *Sir Philip Sidney and the English Renaissance* (London: MacMillan, 1965), especially at pages 23–26, 229–31, 246–48.

30. For a useful survey of issues raised by the interrelations between genre and gender, see M. Gerhart, *Genre Choices Gender Questions* (Norman: University of Oklahoma Press, 1992).

Donne, Decorum, and Truth: Grounds of His Literary Art

Earl Miner

Explaining literary practice and change requires principles with defining power. For Donne these have traditionally included inherited conventions ("Petrarchanism"), subjects (love and religion), and literary kinds. Other criteria have included the relation assumed between the individual and the world ("mode"), gender, and social conceptions. My aim in this essay is not to dismiss those but to consider a dialectic between decorum and truth, the terms of which would have been more recognizable to Donne and his readers than some other concerns. A dialectical approach saves one from the extremes of the same result to every critical inquiry and a wholly different explanation for each poet or poem. The approach does not render explaining easier.[1]

Considering that every sentence is affirmative, negative, or interrogative, truth is a simple matter. But to identify truth in nonlinguistic matters via language is no easy thing, as Donne says in "Satyre III"—"On a huge hill, / Cragged and steep, Truth stands, and hee that will / Reach her, about must, and about must goe" (79–81).[2] Truth, the daughter of time, was held single as well as solitary, and Donne well knew the difficulty of access to her."Seeke true religion. O where?" (43). Something might be true but irrelevant: " 'Tis true, 'tis day, what though it be?" ("Breake of Day," 1). One may want sufficient evidence: "Show me deare Christ, thy spouse so bright and cleare. . . . Is she selfe truth and errs?" (Westmoreland Holy Sonnets 2.1, 6). Fresh discovery and novel terms do not guarantee acceptable results: "Oft from new proofes, and new phrase, new doubts grow" ("To the Countess of Bedford"—"Madame, You have refin'd mee": 65). One of the greatest problems is that human nature, history, and these sad times militate against truth, as Donne emphasizes in his *First Anniversary*:

> 'Tis all in peeces, all cohaerence gone;
> All just supply, and all Relation;
> Prince, Subject, Father, Sonne, are things forgot,
> For every man alone thinkes he hath got
> To be a Phoenix, and that then can bee
> None of that kinde, of which he is, but hee.

> (*P* 213–18)

The new way abolishes distinctions between prince and his subject, between father and his son. (Nominally about a girl's death, this poem conveys its sense of woman's social place by its silences.) It is not by any means the case that truth is the sole problem. The problems of "cohaerence," "just supply," and "relation" are less those of what is or of truth than of what ought to be, of what is fitting: decorum.

Dissonance between the fitting and the true constitutes a major source of Donne's freshness and power. It is declared a truth that "No where / Lives a woman true, and faire" ("Goe, and catche a falling starre," 17–18). Revelation of truth falsifies the decorous. It is not difficult to imagine how Donne might literalize Thomas Campion's "There is a garden in her face." He constructs a face in his elegy, "The Anagram":

> Marry, and love thy *Flavia,* for shee
> Hath all things, whereby others beautious bee,
> For, though her eyes be small, her mouth is great,
> Though they be Ivory, yet her teeth are jeat,
> Though they be dimme, yet she is light enough,
> And though her harsh haire fall, her skinne is rough;
> What though her cheeks be yellow, 'her haire is red,
> Give her thine, and she hath a maydenhead. . . .
> Though all her parts be not in th'usuall place,
> She 'hath yet an Anagram of a good face.

> (1–8, 15–16)

One way of describing what goes on here is to point to the way in which the truth obtainable from a Roman love elegy ("love thy *Flavia*") shatters the decorum of the Renaissance blazon that itemized in partitive fashion a woman's beauties. But the repetition of iconoclastic truth may become conventional, and Donne sometimes is found replacing one decorum by another.

Of course, the situation in which Donne began his poetic career
with satires and elegies was pretty nearly the opposite. The late Tudor
age in which he grew up was so fractured by religious disputes, and
its court politics was so riven by vaunting intrigue, that it is small wonder that the decorous was almost another truth. The strong need to
follow decorum led poets to vie in saying what other gifted poets said,
to confirm (whatever their unruly ambitions) their subscription to the
honied conceits of "Petrarchan" rhyme and courtly codes of reason.
As Spenser showed, many a Colin Clout went home again from court
in disillusion. Yet his return took him back on the Arcadian way.
Donne's satires, even the third on religion, pointedly, even empirically
deal with social perils and struggles at court.

Certain things here deserve emphasis. Donne's satires speak with
open, bitter rudeness, violating any expectations of pastoralism
(which was often used for covert satire). That is, for him the old decorous ways will not stand scrutiny by a severer test of truth. It is equally
important that one realize, however, that the new, exposing truth still
requires a decorum. The piping on "th'Oaten Flute" suitable to pastoral yields to the appropriately harsh satire.

In "Satyre IV," the unnamed accoster of the speaker holds forth
with bitter accusations:

> He names a price for every office paid;
> He saith, our warres thrive ill, because delai'd;
> That offices are entail'd, and that there are
> Perpetuities of them, lasting as farre
> As the last day; And that great officers,
> Doe with the Pirates share, and Dunkirkers.
> Who wasts in meat, in clothes, in horse, he notes;
> Who loves Whores, who boyes, and who goats.

> (S 121–28)

The climactic, lurid last line caps, and almost distracts from, the bitter
social criticism of the court system. And yet it is not nearly as explosive as some details in the invective of "Satyre II," especially in the
account of those elementary violations of truth, lies. They lie,

> to'every suitor lye in every thing,
> Like a Kings favorite, yea like a King;
> . . . more shamelesse farre
> Then carted whores, lye, to the grave Judge; for

Bastardy'abounds not in Kings titles, nor
Symonie'and Sodomy in Churchmens lives,
As these things do in him; by these he thrives.

(S 69–70, 72–76)

Donne seeks some safer distance in writing about kings rather than a
queen. But as all knew, the then aged Elizabeth I had had to live out
her reign with the charge of bastardy. There is no garden in that face
whitened with lead paint. If publicly known, these lines might have
cost Donne dearly. His saving plea is the nowadays less familiar justification by classical convention. Satires I and IV are variations on the
satire by Horace most often imitated in the seventeenth century (S
1.9, "Ibam forte via sacra"), in which Horace reports his being ac-
costed on the Via Sacra by a bore who pesters him for a good word
with his patron, Maecenas. Today there seems a wide gap between
the lighter touch of Horace and the explosive charges by Donne. But
to an age of rigid class and gender hierarchies, to challenge assumptions was even more radical than challenging by words. Very often
decorum seemed another kind of truth.

George Puttenham's *Arte of English Poesie* deals with "Ornament Poeticall" in the first chapter of the third book. It should cause no surprise that he implicitly uses the art-nature distinction to treat the old
trope of art as dress to extend a comparison for poetry with "great
Madames of honour":

be they for personage or otherwise never so comely and bewtifull, yet if
they want [lack] their courtly habillements or at leastwise such other ap-
parell as custome and civilitie have ordained to cover their naked bodies
. . . even so cannot our vulgar [English-language] Poesie shew it selfe either
gallant or gorgious, if any limme be left naked and bare and not clad in his
kindly clothes and colours.[3]

Toward the end of that chapter there is an anticipation of Donne's
"Anagram." If poets use the colors (embellishments) in ways

not well tempered, or not well layd, or be used in excesse, or never so little
disordered or misplaced . . . but rather do disfigure the stuffe and spill the
whole workmanship, taking away all bewtie and good liking from it, no
lesse then if the crimson tainte, which should be laid upon a Ladies lips or
right in the center of her cheekes, should by some oversight or mishap be

applied to her forhead or chinne, it would make . . . but a very ridiculous bewtie.[4]

Puttenham shows that in "The Anagram" Donne uses what he holds to be true of Flavia to convey her violation of decorum, and that just as her departure from amatory decorum reveals the repellant satiric truth about her, the veracity conforms to another, reinforcing satiric decorum.

Donne violates old decorums to reveal new truths—and new decorums. It was impossible to conceive of any feature of verbal expression not subject to that rule. As Puttenham puts it, "our speach asketh one maner of *decencie* in respect of the person who speakes, another of his to whom it is spoke, another of whom we speake, another of what we speake, and in what place or time and to what purpose."[5] Decorum, what Puttenham and writers to Milton and Dryden term decency, applies to all factors of utterance. It is inevitable and, Milton held, "is the grand master peece to observe."[6]

One reason why "ornament" has no such power over our minds today is that our ideological assumptions differ from those of Puttenham, Donne, and others of those times. Puttenham insists that "in speaking or writing of a Princes affaires & fortunes there is a certain *Decorum,* that we may not use the same termes in their busnes as we might very wel doe in a meaner person." The plain fact is that the chief differentiation, whether of persons of genres, is hierarchical. Any doubt about the basically conservative nature of decorum is dispelled by the bludgeoning insistence of Thomas Rymer. In *The Tragedies of the Last Age Consider'd* (1678), he drastically faults Beaumont and Fletcher's *Maid's Tragedy.* "Tragedy," he declares, "cannot represent a woman without modesty as natural and essential to her." If in historical fact "a woman has got . . . impudence," she must be dismissed from the dignity of the tragic theater to comedy.[8] Rymer is particularly upset by the killing of the king in the play. (Charles I had been executed in 1649, three decades before.) Also,

> I question whether in Poetry a King can be an accessary to a crime. . . . If I mistake not, in Poetry no woman is to kill a man, except her quality gives her the advantage above him, nor is a Servant to kill the Master, nor a Private Man, much less a Subject, to kill a King, nor on the contrary.[9]

It should be noted that although women are thought lower than men, that presumes the same social level. If the "person" of the woman is

superior to that of a man, she may be shown to kill him. Social rank
supersedes gender.

Social decorums—distinctions of rank, hierarchy, degree—
mattered to an extent that we are hard-pressed to understand.
Donne's unsanctioned marriage to Anne More was the major violation
of decorum in his life. Her social rank was higher than his (not to mention that her guardian was his master, Sir Thomas Egerton). He
quickly saw the inside of a prison and, with this lesson in "decency,"
he came to devise more decorous ways to deal with the great ladies
who were his patronesses. Here in its entirety is a letter (written before
1614) to Lucy, Countess of Bedford:

Madam,

Amongst many other dignities which this letter hath by being received
and seen by you, it is not the least, that it was prophesied of before it was
born: for your brother told you in his letter that I had written: he did me
much honour both in advancing my truth so farre as to call a promise an
act already done; and to provide me with a means of doing him a service
in this act, which is but doing right to myself: for by this performance of
mine own word, I have justified that part of his Letter which concerned
me; and it had been a double guiltinesse in me to have made him guilty
towards you. It makes no difference that this came not the same day, nor
bears the same date as his; for though in inheritances and worldly possessions we consider the dates of Evidences, yet in Letters, by which we de-
liver over our affections, and assurances of friendship, and the best
faculties of our souls, times and daies cannot have interest, nor be considerable, because that which passes by them, is eternall, and out of the measure of time. Because therefore it is the office of this Letter, to convey my
best wishes, and all the effects of a noble love unto you, (which are the
best fruits that so poor a soil, as my poor soul is, can produce) you may be
pleased to allow the Letter thus much of the souls privilege, as to exempt it
from straitnesse of hours, or any measure of times, and so beleeve it came
then. And for my part, I shall make it so like my soul, that as that affection,
of which it is the messenger, began in me without my knowing when, any
more than I know when my soul began: so it shall continue as long as that.

Your most affextionate friend and servant,
J. D.

(*L*, letter 9)

Witty as it is, this letter is that rare creation by Donne, something
without any ascertainable meaning beyond notice of itself: a letter of
devoted feeling ("most affextionate") mentioned to the noble lady by

her brother, the second Lord Harrington (d. February 1614). Only wild guesses go any farther: his closeness to her brother? A reminder of "worldly possessions" (i.e., a hint about financial support)? Its fulfillment of duty ("office") to her? Given her credit for wit with him and Jonson, it is quite possible that, in the terms used here, he expected her to smile at a witty, messageless letter. Its sole evident truth is its decorum, its preference of "decency" over meaning. If she understood that truth defined as decorum, she is doubly witty. If her understanding did not reach that far, she would still understand the epistolary and social truth of the time that a noble title should be said to coincide with exalted spirits.

Of course, that which was so persistently true by convention was constantly belied by experience, and panegyric needed justifying. There were certain venerable excuses. Perhaps the most widely used apology was that one exceeded truth in order to set an ideal version for the actual person to use as a model for improvement. Jonson cleverly used this to make a panegyric point when the excuse was not needed, in "An epistle to Master John Selden." Here was somebody whom all seem to have thought entitled to high praise: there could not be a safer, more decorous time to confess one's error:

> Though I confesse (as every Muse hath err'd,
> And mine not least) I have too oft preferr'd
> Men past their termes, and prais'd some names too much,
> But 'twas with purpose to have made them such.
>
> (19–22)[10]

The confession seems to guarantee veracious integrity.

In Jonson's "Epistle to Sir Edward Sacville, Now Earle of Dorset" the method emerges identifiabley in two lines: "For benefits are ow'd with the same mind / As they are done, and such returnes they find" (5–6). The meticulous, bartering balance of the lines conveys a need to define just what is right in the matter of doing well. Although bearing the marks of Jonson's coinage, his "benefits" surely draws on Seneca's "De Beneficiis," in which the giver has responsibilities exactly equal to those of the receiver. "No! Gifts and thankes should have one cheerfull face, / So each, that's done, and tane, becomes a Brace" (39–40)—the "done" and the taken are poised by the caesura-marking syntax to become the even or double pair of the "Brace." Defining, discriminating, knowing the other in the pair, knowing oneself as one in a pair of benefits—these define the properly human.

Donne's awareness of the problem is shown by a passage from his verse letter, "To the Countess of Huntingdon" ("Man to Gods image"):

> If you can think these flatteries, they are,
>   For then your judgement is below my praise,
> If they were so, oft, flatteries worke as farre,
>   As Counsels, and as farre th'endeavour raise.
>
> So my ill reaching you might there grow good,
>   But I remaine a poyson'd fountaine still;
> But not your beauty, vertue, knowledge, blood
>   Are more above all flattery, then my will.
>
> And if I flatter you, 'tis not you
>   But my own judgment, which did long agoe
> Pronounce, that all these praises should be true,
>   And vertue should your beauty, 'and birth outgrow.
>
> (49–60)

Like Jonson, Donne seems in some sense tortured with the literal syntax of his writing and the figurative one of his exact ethical calculation; I . . . you, you . . . my owne (pronounce) praises . . . true, virtue [outgrows] beauty + virtue. But the seeming balance is illusory. The larger syntax allows her to speak conditionally: she does so by showing herself wrong. His will surpasses her best qualities. Flattery of her ("you") derives from his reasoning power ("judgment"), which long ago prophesied that anything he said would be true.

A striking characteristic of Donne's poetry is its absorption or adaptation of one sphere of experience by another. Students often say that he uses matters of love or sex in his religious poetry, and of religion in his love poetry. Those things are sometimes true. But it is more accurate to say that he identifies the disparities between the claims of decorum and truth, both within and between differing spheres. Decorum is a necessity for, and therefore also a product of, human interrelations in social and public dealings. Truth, on the other hand, both transcends those interrelations in time and history and reduces to depths of individual experience. The poets preceding Donne had so socialized the world of private experience that their understanding was ripe for a radical review of its heavily decorous "ornament" by a poet who would insist on the standard of truth. Unlike Jonson, who continued to prize the social definition of experience (and was even more vocal about truth), Donne often established the separate, inner, private experience as the locus of value.

One of the best illustrations is offered by "The Indifferent," in which with male bravado the speaker declares his ability to love any woman, "so she be not true." Truth or fidelity in love had naturally been taken as its central, decorous virtue. Here the truth is taken to be sexual promiscuity: Venus swears "by Loves sweetest Part, Variety" (20). Fidelity is one of the "old vices" (12) left over from a social world of "mothers." Dependent as it is on extravagance, such wit cannot easily be made to serve yet larger purposes without some major adjustment. Donne normally achieves larger purposes either by verbal paradox or by so radically locating his values in the world of private love or religion that the social and public worlds become outside, alien alterities.

Something of the world of the satires is recalled in many of the love poems, for the evident reason that judgment is passed on the outer world by an individual. In "The Sunne Rising," the imperious lover bids the sun,

> goe chide
> Late schoole boyes, and sowre prentices,
> Goe tell Court-huntsmen, that the King will ride,
> Call country ants to harvest offices.

(5–8)

Something could be made of Donne's dismissal of the peasantry here. But his sense of the decorum and truth in this matter does not differ from the attitudes of other poets of the time. Rather, we should note in what follows how the claims of the private world absorb those of the social and public. It is not normal to hector (from within the curtains of the beds of the time) a personified sun for shining through a chink in the drapes. "Looke," the male lover orders, and learn that the East and West Indies along with the world's kings lie "All here in one bed" (20). The process works in major part by transferring experience and values from the outer worlds to the private world of lovers abed. That charges the human, amatory microcosm with the significance of a macrocosm admitted on the microcosmic terms, greatly enriching the separate, the individual ("idios," "privatus"). There are limits, however, as the poem's drift into solipsistic claims shows.

> She'is all States, and all Princes, I,
>> Nothing else is.
> Princes doe but play us; compar'd to this,
> All honor's mimique; All wealth alchimie.

(21–24)

There is an undeniable thrill in this (undeniably male) claim. But finally there simply cannot be sufficient truth in the reversal of the old decorum celebrating the microcosm for its reflection of the macrocosm. The very claim that validates their value of love abed—that she is all states and he all princes—quite simply requires that much else be.

Obviously, enormous tensions and strains mark Donne's poetry and assist in providing the excitement one feels in reading it. But there is a fundamental problem that is revealed by attention to the dialectic of truth and decorum. The energy necessary to expose false decorum, the power to reveal truth, derives from a naysaying that is variously manifested but that can most simply be named satire. In this representative sense "satire" includes wit, conceits, surprise, inversions, and sudden shifts or transpositions. Given his complex manipulations of decorum and his constant threatening of the stability of truth with paradox, it is remarkable how convinced we are that we know what he means, that we can hear his voice. When we stand as it were just within earshot, it may be difficult to believe that he could do what he does. The most famous instance is probably "A Hymne to God the Father." We may abbreviate his three stanzas to define the issues.

> Wilt thou forgive that sin where I begunne . . .
>> When thou has done, thou has not done,
>>> For, I have more.
>>>> *
> Wilt thou forgive that sin by which I wonne
>> Others to sin? . . .
>>> When thou hast done, thou hast not done,
>>>> For, I have more.
>>>>> *
> I have a sinne of feare, that when I have spunne
>> My last thred, I shall perish on the shore . . .
>>> And, having done that, Thou hast done,
>>>> I have no more.

The smooth, singsong rhythm of this "Hymne" honors a simpler decorum for musical setting observed in a number of Donne's songs. Cer-

tain other possible theatrics are also muted in the religious decorum
as Donne moves stanza by stanza from original sin to personal sin to
reliance on God's mercy. That much is also an untroubled truth. The
counterforce of the poem comes from a gesture that, abstractly considered, could only be distasteful: a mere wordplay on his own name.
What could be more indecorous for the holy occasion? The disruption
works only because it emphasizes the truth of the conditions most essential to the poem: who speaks about what. It is Donne, and it is
"done" on the crucial Christian issue, his eternal salvation.

Another of the most familiar of his divine poems may be poised
against that simpler melodic line. The 1633 Sonnet 10, "Batter my
heart, three person'd God," is as explosively masochistic as the other
poem is lightly confident. Even before feminist criticism, the violent
paradox of the conclusion engaged attention: "for I / Except you' en-
thrall mee, never shall be free, / Nor ever chast, except you ravish
mee." Although "ravish" and even "rape" need not designate sexual
assault in the seventeenth century, the dependence here of chastity
on being ravished sets the stark assumption clearly before us.

Our understanding may be heightened by a triangulation involving
this sonnet and two poems by Thomas Carew. His "Elegie" on Donne
has a parenthetical passage that provides one gloss on the metaphor
at issue.

> But the flame
> Of thy brave Soule, (that shot such heat and light,
> As burnt our earth, and made our darknesse bright,
> Committed holy Rapes upon our Will,
> Did through the eye the melting heart distill;
> And the deepe knowledge of darke truths so teach,
> As sense might judge, what phansie could not reach;)
> Must be desir'd for ever.
>
> (14–21)[11]

The central concept in this complex passage is that of the heat-light
of Donne's ardency, which uses our more elementary capacities (the
melting heart of feeling rather than the eye of reason; sense rather
than imagination) for the greatest spiritual effects: "holy Rapes upon
our Will." This also treads too close to the idea of pleasurable rape.
The third poem need not be quoted. Carew's immensely popular sexual fantasy, "The Rapture," imagines intercourse and orgasm (the rap-

ture). In this poem the metaphors (e.g., phallic rudder) convey features of the sexual experience undergone rather than using sexual experience as a metaphor for religious experience. Given certain common assumptions, Carew's erotic detail is more decorous than Donne's!

With Donne's sonnet, his truths and ours—as well as his fitnesses and ours—require more complex adjustment. He has sexual ravishment in mind as a traditional mystical metaphor. More important still, this cry to God is but the last version of efforts to define an individual's desperate calling for divine presence. He wishes to be battered to be remade, to be overthrown that he may stand, destroyed to be made new (1–4). The sestet (9–14) speaks of love, betrothal, and marriage—and, in that context, ravishment belongs to the initial marriage bed. The intervening lines harmonize what precedes with what follows by use of the military-civil conceit of the soul's danger in captivity, betrayal, and rule by a usurper. The full coherence of the metaphors gives them their propriety and significance. The coherence imparts a control to the fissive, centrifugal Donnean force of personality by an equal harmony of decorum in the propriety and truth in the significance.

We can see that the energy characterized as satire diminishes in the religious poems, just as it is weakened in lyrics such as "Sweetest love, I do not goe, / For wearinesse of thee." The satire diminishes, that is, to the extent that Donne accepts the truth of the ordinary decorums of poetry, whether of love, religion, or praise. It is obvious that such poems do not have the power of "Batter my heart, three person'd God." Their lessening of power derives from the attenuation of committed intelligence and of those energies here typified as satire.

Donne also wrote religious poems more complex than the hymn considered and more normal than the sonnet. One such is the "Hymne to God my God, in my sicknesse," much of whose conception and imagery make comparison with that holy sonnet an illuminating exercise. But "Goodfriday, 1613. Riding Westward" is like none of Donne's other divine poems, and I find it difficult to think of an equivalent among his secular ones. I accept it for what Donne purports it to be, a meditation on that holy day as the poet rides toward the west, even while his "Soules forme bends toward the East" (10) and the imagined crucifixion. There is paradox, but it is contained. If his soul turned east, "There I should see a Sunne, by rising set, / And by that setting endlesse day beget" (11–12). Here too there is a pun, on "a Sunne" and the Son. (Not even Donne will so risk decorum here as to

enter the further rhyme of this "Sunne" with his own name.) The possible explosive power of paradox is fully contained by being made part
of the Christian mysteries of the Trinity and the Incarnation: "What a
death were it then to see God dye?" (18). To witness the death of the
incarnate Son, member of the triune deity, would indeed be "What a
death"—that is, death for the (immortal) soul of the speaker. For it is
only the incarnate form of the Son that dies. Deity cannot and does
not die, as the prayer or address of the last seven lines shows: "O Savi-
our, as thou hang'st upon the tree" (36). To me this poem merits the
name of his most effective poetic narrative.

It could not be so successful without an assurance of decorum and
truth that Donne seldom achieved in narrative. Even in "Goodfriday,
1613," the success of the narrative depends upon its being held to a
minimum. The same holds for poems as different from it as from each
other: "The Blossom," "The Extasie," "The Flea," and "Twicknam
Garden." The success of the narrative requires its being dominated by
the intense presence of lyric. In this (if not all things) Herbert is very
similar. He succeeds in poems such as "The Flower" and "The Collar"
with what seem narratives slightly more sustained than Donne's. But
his longer, fuller narratives ("The Church-Porch," "The Sacrifice," and
"The Church Militant") also pose problems.

Although none match his lyrics in success, Donne's attempts at
longer narrative vary somewhat in nature. Essentially there are two
kinds of poems: panegyrics and satires. (Poems like his epigrams simply have no need to be narrative.) The more purely panegyric poems
provide the traditional obverse of satire, using many of the same
"places" or motifs: birth or origins, deeds, testimony by others, the
"ethical proof" of the poetic speaker's testimony, and so on. Panegyric's amplification resembles satire's diminution in possessing such
strong decorous claims that narrative is dispossessed: the claim calls
to its service both decorum and truth. Or, to describe matters another
way, rhetoric displaces narrative. Narrative may be called upon to establish the place of people and times, as with *narratio* in an oration.
But it is a temporary resource, a means rather than an end.

Spenser provides a highly useful counterpoint. In *The Faerie Queene,*
there is an almost profligate enjoyment or dispensing of plot from "A
Gentle Knight was pricking on the plaine." That may seem to be a
narrative nowhere, but its insistent, sustained narrative preterit is not
Donnean. Neither is Spenser's great truth preoccupation, distinguishing what seems from what is—Duessa from Fidessa, true from false

Florimel, one "Sansboy" from another, the Garden of Adonis from the Bower of Bliss, and so going on and on, for the prime narrative reason that only what continues to happen reveals the truth. Just as Donne's dominantly satiric longer poems have narrative moments, Spenser often halts his narrative for a lyric *descriptio,* a panegyric of Elizabeth I, or a diatribe against Catholicism. But these are as traditional in heroic narrative as a *narratio* is in an oration pro or contra. Moreover, Spenser does have poems that reflect the needs Donne sought to satisfy in longer poems. Narrative may be exiguous for him as well. It is largely excluded in his "Mother Hubberd's Tale" by satire, in his "Astrophel" by panegyric, and in his "Colin Clouts Come Home Again" by a mixture of both.

The most revealing as well as most interesting of Donne's longer poems are his two "Anniversaries" of the death of Elizabeth Drury and "The Progresse of the Soul." It is striking that he relies so heavily on stanza-like, lyric-like units, that he seeks to adjust his usual lyric affirmation to satiric antagonism. In fact, with Donne an emphatic move toward narrative almost guarantees satire. (One textual line of "The Progresse of the Soul" has the title, "Poema Satiricum / Metempsycosis.") His satires are not fully narrative any more than most verse satires, but they and his more lightly satiric elegies, such as "The Perfume," constitute his greatest triumphs in use of narrative. This seems quite idiosyncratic or at least special to Donne, if we think of the narrative triumphs lying ahead. But Ben Jonson's single outright narrative, "The Famous Voyage" (down London's main sewer ditch) is not read with pleasure. Jonson's sharing of Donne's problem reveals that the ability to devise a fictional plot is not involved. *The Alchemist* alone gloriously disproves that. Other features of narrative must be involved.

Insofar as those features relate to truth and decorum, they involve continuous credibility of events, whether taken for themselves or as representing such another scheme as in Spenser's allegory. The "Anniversaries" do not, however, have continuous events, and they lack credibility. The death of a girl (Elizabeth Drury) provides a decorous occasion for panegyric but not for a simultaneous satire of almost apocalyptic proportions on the world left without her. The basic conception satisfies neither the requirements of decorum nor standards for credible truth. The magic possible for Donne in his coruscating lyrics will not endure magnification into narrative.

There are many kinds of literary adequacy and inadequacy, however. Both "Anniversaries" have many moving passages. For them one can put up with a good deal. They possess an intellectual seriousness that inoculates us from offenses of excess in decorum and deficiency in truth. That cannot be said either of Donne's "Progress of the Soul" or Jonson's "Famous Voyage." Donne seems to have realized as much and to have halted a progress that was doomed. If, as some have thought, he planned to take that obscene soul to Elizabeth I, his breaking off was an act of self-preserving prudence. Jonson saw his "Voyage" to its end. His failure is that of a bad joke. In some sense, both poets were attempting the mock heroic without the resources to sustain its mixed decorum or its ironic truth. Both poets were creators of lyrics, satires, and panegyrics.

They brilliantly show how they could sustain satire and praise in lyrics. That fact should remind us that lyric is not the tender flower that some think it to be. Lyric can interrupt narrative and drama, as they can interrupt each other. Neither narrative nor drama can interrupt lyric, however, and it alone cannot interrupt itself. This most hardy smaller plant can absorb so much else and yet retain its integrity. One should not be surprised, therefore, that it was as a lyric poet that Donne performed his miracles in handling the most difficult feats straining decorum and putting truth to the test. There and in the other kingdom of the sermon he reigned as monarch of wit.

NOTES

1. Exigencies of publication have not permitted full scholarly and critical commentary. That will be supplied in a book-length version of this essay, which is forthcoming.

2. The works of John Donne are quoted from the following editions (abbreviations and page references are found in the text):

> D *The Divine Poems,* ed. Helen Gardner (Oxford: Clarendon, 1959)
> E *The Elegies and the Songs and Sonnets,* ed. Helen Gardner (Oxford: Clarendon, 1965)
> L *Letters to Severall Persons of Honour,* ed. Charles Edmund Merrill, Jr. (New York: Sturgis & Walton, 1910)
> P *The Poems,* ed. Herbert J. C. Grierson, 2 vols. (Oxford: Clarendon, 1958)
> S *The Satires, Epigrams and Verse Letters,* ed. W. Milgate (Oxford: Clarendon, 1967).

3. George Puttenham, quoted in G. Gregory Smith, ed., *Elizabethan Critical Essays* (Oxford: Clarendon, 1904), 2:142; spelling modernized.

4. Puttenham, in Smith, *Elizabethan Critical Essays*, 2:143.

5. Puttenham, in Smith, *Elizabethan Critical Essays*, 2:175.

6. John Milton, *Complete Prose Works*, ed. Douglas Bush, et al. (New Haven: Yale University Press, 1959), 2:405.

7. Puttenham, in Smith, *Elizabethan Critical Essays*, 2:177.

8. Thomas Rymer, in J. E. Spingarn, ed., *Critical Essays of the Seventeenth Century* (Bloomington: Indiana University Press, 1963), 2:194.

9. Rymer, in Spingarn, *Critical Essays of the Seventeenth Century*, 2:195.

10. Ben Jonson's poems are quoted from *The Complete Poetry*, ed. William B. Hunter, Jr. (New York: Norton, 1963).

11. Thomas Carew's poems are quoted from *The Poems*, ed. Rhodes Dunlap (Oxforfd: Clarendon, 1957).

WORKS CITED

Carew, Thomas. *The Poems*. Edited by Rhodes Dunalp. Oxford: Clarendon, 1957.

Donne, John. *Letters to Severall Persons of Honour*. Edited by Charles Edmund Merrill, Jr. New York: Sturgis & Walton, 1910.

———. *The Divine Poems*. Edited by Helen Gardner. Oxford: Clarendon, 1959.

———. *The Elegies and the Songs and Sonnets*. Edited by Helen Gardner. Oxford: Clarendon, 1965.

———. *The Poems (with Anniversaries)*. Edited by Herbert J. C. Grierson. 2 vols. Oxford: Clarendon, 1958.

———. *The Satires, Epigrams and Verse Letters (including The Progress of the Soul)*. Edited by W. Milgate. Oxford: Clarendon, 1967.

Herbert, George. *The Works*. Edited by F. E. Hutchinson. Oxford: Clarendon, 1953.

Jonson, Ben. *The Complete Poetry of Ben Jonson*. Edited by William B. Hunter, Jr. New York: Norton, 1963.

Milton, John. *Complete Prose Works*. Edited by Douglas Bush, et al., Vol. 2. New Haven: Yale University Press, 1959.

Smith, G. Gregory, ed. *Elizabethan Critical Essays (including Puttenham)*. 2 vols. Oxford: Clarendon, 1904.

Spenser, Edmund. *The Poetical Works*. Edited by J. C. Smith and E. de Selincourt. London: Oxford University Press, 1950.

Spingarn, J. E., ed. *Critical Essays of the Seventeenth Century*. 3 vols. Bloomington: Indiana University Press, 1963.

Mannerist Donne: Showing Art in the Descriptive Verse Epistles and the Elegies

L. E. Semler

RHETORICAL, ORATORICAL, POETICAL, AND VISUAL THEORIES AND TERMI-
nologies, while maintaining their own distinctness, cross-fertilize one
another from antiquity onwards—with the result that many common
words possess multiple resources of meaning. Terms such as "invention," "figure," and "history" (to cite three of the most relevant) are
granted related, analogous, and also strikingly distinct meanings depending on the theoretical context by which they are interpreted. The
following examination of some of Donne's poems will allow nonvisual
formal legacies a natural enrichment derived from aesthetic meanings
accessible to Donne in the 1590s.

In the volume *Poems, By J.D. With Elegies on the Authors Death*
(1633), the descriptive verse epistles, clearly pendant poems, "The Storme" and "The Calme," precede the collection of complimentary poetic letters. While distinct in itself, the pair crucially prepares the
reader for the experience of the following poems. And not just in practice, but also in theory, for "The Storme" commences with an eight-
line introduction that says much about Donne's aesthetic:

> Thou which art I, ('tis nothing to be soe)
> Thou which art still thy selfe, by these shalt know
> Part of our passage; And, a hand, or eye
> By *Hilliard* drawne, is worth an history,
> By a worse painter made; and (without pride)
> When by thy judgment they are dignifi'd,
> My lines are such. 'Tis the preheminence
> Of friendship onely to'impute excellence.[1]

Much may be deduced from this. Lines 3–5 rely on a basic opposition
between miniature portraiture (that is, limning) and usually large-scale

40

narrative painting (Alberti's *istoria*; in England called "histories" or "story-work"). Driving this mini-*paragone* debate is the self-conscious Elizabethan fascination with and undeniable expertise in limning and works "in little" despite the mainstream continental development of works "in great."[2] While the Italians work hard to perfect the invention of the *istoria* of each painting, the English art treatises stoutly defend their best native miniaturists as inventors and executors worthy of comparison with continental masters. And the English argument should be not unintelligible to the Italians, for it runs along commonly accepted lines: just as an *istoria* is to be enriched by the presence of various praiseworthy arrangements, figural positions and evocations of "the life," so too a miniature portrait requires its virtuoso inventions and expressive liveliness.

Both narrative painting and miniature portraiture participate in the *difficultà:facilità* formula: that is, there are technical and aesthetic difficulties peculiar to (and others also shared by) each of these forms of painting that, when attempted and carried off with apparently effortless grace and skill, constitute shows of virtuosity—visual *sprezzatura*.[3] One of the defining traits of mannerist art is the high priority given to the invention, presentation, and "conquest" of such parades of artistry. The artist strives to work into his artifact a number of these stunning displays of technical skill that not only strain the ostensible subject of the artwork but also push at the very limits of the medium. The targeted audience, those who know the art and its attendant difficulties, balances and resolves the *difficultà:facilità* equation by responding to the virtuosity of the artist with superlatives of praise. Thus, the *difficultà* are invented, presented, recognized, and affirmed; the cycle is completed only to begin again in what may be considered an overbreeding of virtuosity, an ultrarefinement of artifice.

Sheer size allows large-scale painting innumerable possibilities for the expression of the *difficultà:facilità* formula, while limning and related forms of miniaturism make a virtue of necessity, turning constraints of space to their advantage, accentuating the virtuosity of the performance in inverse proportion to availability of performance space. It is, after all, in Donne's words, "harder to make a little clocke, a little picture, any thing in a little, then in a larger forme."[4] Drummond of Hawthornden puts it nicely: "a wise Painter showeth in a small Pourtrait more ingine than in a great."[5] The showing of "ingine" is exactly the point.

In his theory (*The Art of Limning*), Hilliard identifies the representation of the eye and the hand as two of the most significant difficulties to be overcome by the studious workman and a look at any number of his portraits confirms his mastery of these problems. The hands must appear elegantly graceful and yet unaffected, and like the eyes they must be realistic and suggestive of life and motion. When Donne acknowledges these *difficultà* and credits them with the value of an entire (albeit lesser) narrative painting, he enacts his participation in the *difficultà:facilità* formula, reveals his knowledge of how to judge an Hilliardian miniature and, at a more submerged level, stands up for the intrinsic value of the English miniaturist tradition.

Donne's reference to this hermeneutic-eulogistic system is instantly both analogical and prescriptive. "The Storme," and I would add "The Calme," represent only "part" of his passage ("The Storme," l. 3): like the Hilliardian eye or hand, these poems constitute an expression of artistic virtuosity. Donne's selection of this particular poetic genre for this exercise makes good sense given the general recognition of this form as something of a poetic performance space.[6] The "calm and storm" poetic tradition may be regarded as an expansion of Puttenham's figure of cronographia (and possibly topographia)—that is, a form of *descriptio*—and related to the third form of ancient oratory, the epideictic speech, an artful and polished showpiece constructed for the pleasure of the auditors.[7] As Hilliard determines to conquer artistic *difficultà* and to have his work judged by the standard of facility of executed invention, so Donne will lay before Christopher Brooke a display of poetic skill and expect his friend to judge the poems according to the vibrance and ingenuity of their wit, in overall design and in details. All Donne's complimentary verse letters function within the aesthetic ecosystem of Mannerism: they are poems of devoted praise, witty self-abasement, and ingenious display passing to and fro between friends.

The mannerist aesthetic cultivates *artificio* to the degree that the strictures governing the representation of *natura* are severely modified. However, this tireless—for further rarefication is always possible in a milieu of superlatives and "perfections"—and treacherous—for one could at any time simply fail and thus stain one's work with affectation—struggle for beautiful style (*bella maniera*), as artificial as it patently is, occurs within a long humanistic tradition of mimetic art in which the inner spiritual and emotional states of the depicted figures are to be revealed in their outward gestures and expressions. The growth of Mannerism within this affective tradition makes for some wonderful compromises between mimetic expressiveness and the most rarefied artifice, compromises that push much farther into the realm of overt artifice than the principles of classic art ever allowed. Hilliard's expertise in this style is seen in his fusion of these two impulses. "The Storme" and "The Calme" each shows this dual commitment to the expression of inner state in the leading figures and to the demonstration of the most extreme and self-conscious artifice.

The marriage of the literary form of complimentary verse letter with the Mannerist aesthetic's focus on affective expressiveness modified by intense artifice could not be happier. And one might not unreasonably suggest that it was Donne's attraction to the creative embodiment of such Mannerist principles that led to his invention of the verse epistle as such a paradoxical and fine artifact of love and self-love, genuine expressiveness and sheer artistic virtuosity, real-world meaning and absence of meaning outside the realm of poetic artifice. Donne tells us and Brooke how to read his poems and preempts our response by demanding what is only natural within the tradition of friendship literature. For friendship, too, is an art of superlatives, of hyperbolic praise and devotion, of performance and response. Without pride (line 5), Donne can rely on his friendship with Brooke to guarantee Brooke's favorable response to the poem(s). He will trust Brooke as a friend "to'impute excellence" and thereby make these "lines" what they are, the equal of exquisite Hilliardian *difficultà*. Here again, the Mannerist aesthetic and the courtly tradition of complimentary friendship verse dovetail together; the former demanding Donne's presentation of his artifact in terms of its *difficultà* and the latter demanding his literary self-abasement (line 1) and utter dependence on Brooke's enacted friendship.

There is no doubt that "The Storme" and "The Calme" function as a pair, with the latter continuing and intensifying the concerns of the former. Following the prelude in "The Storme," Donne provides a carefully modulated narrative of the rising storm at sea. The increasing intensity of the storm carries the story from the physical to the metaphysical: a specific material situation presented via a generalized genre metamorphoses into a symbol of psychic nightmare, cronographia becomes the vehicle of a disabling skepticism. On a simple level of story this progression may be regarded as the narrative of the diptych. The representations of the crew, passengers, sea and sky and the speaking persona cooperate to enact this invented *istoria*. In fulfilment of the *ut pictura poesis* tradition, affective representations of

human figures function as focal points of the overall invention or design in which they are subordinated.

However, as should be expected from the prelude and from the poetic genre, "The Storme" and "The Calme" constitute a compendium
of tropes and figures. The narrative fabric is thickly woven of literary
figures from the very first line to the last, with no "plain space" between figures: prosopopeia, ploce, paroemion (alliteration), amplifi-
catio, auxesis, metaphor, meiosis, omiosis (simile), hypotiposis,
antithesis, interogatio, cadence, apostrophe, paronomasia, hyperbole,
and paradox, to cite only the most obvious. The focal points are myr-
iad: far-fetched metaphors, graceful and complicated arrangements of
poetic figures, striking displays of invention or wit. The desire of the
Mannerist artist to fill his art-space with every conceivable expression
of artistic virtuosity regularly results in an artifact in which the ostensible narrative story is overwhelmed by the relentless display of various
figural and other *difficultà*. This occurs as much in Isaac Oliver's brilliant figural drawings, such as *Moses Striking the Rock* (pre-1586), *The
Lamentation over the Dead Christ* (1586), and *The Adoration of the Magi*
(post-1596), as in continental narrative paintings by Vasari, Bronzino,
and Perino del Vaga.[8] It is significant that works of this style—in which
the ostensible narrative as well as the perspectival and architectonic
contexts are subordinated to a marvellous abundance of specific *difficultà*—receive genuine critical commendation from writers such as
Vasari and Aretino. These artworks, visual or literary, are self-conscious about their own artifice and artists praise and imitate each other's key expressions of invention in exactly the way Donne cites
Hilliard's hand and eye, and other poets sequester Donne's best inventions.[9] This leads to a recurring Mannerist paradox, a paradox that
makes appreciation of the Mannerist artifact from the more decorous
reference point of classicism difficult: invention does not simply ornament or play midwife to the *istoria* but remains as the *istoria*; the story
the design tells is the story of design itself.

In other words, the *istoria* of "The Storme" and "The Calme" functions dualistically: on the more traditional level, it is a narrative composed of expressive representations of human figures; while on the
level of higher artifice, it is a rich tapestry of poetic figures. This is
exactly the paradox found in the best of continental Mannerist painting and sculpture: the homage to reality found in the venerable humanistic tradition of visual art is compromised and destabilized by the
simultaneous presence of a new mimesis, that of artifice itself. Portrai-

ture and religious narrative painting feel the tension at its most exquisite: is the artist celebrating the subject (sitter, patron, God, faith) or artifice itself? Put shortly, the question of who or what the subject is, is made simultaneously unavoidable and undecidable: the verse epistle as Donne develops it carries this aesthetic burden perfectly. However, in "The Storme" and "The Calme" both impulses are interwoven and lead to one end. I'll deal with each in turn.

The represented history of these maritime experiences becomes a portrait of the central character, the speaking persona. The affective force of the narrative (the characters' terror, confusion, and dismay) is distilled to its neatest form in the representation of the speaker himself. The chaos of the storm swirls around this poem's central line, which epitomizes the inner state of its chief figure: "But when I wakt, I saw, that I saw not" (line 37). The speaker's experience is characterized by a loss of order, orientation, and distinction, and a subjection to the paradoxical, lonely, and violent. The poem presents itself as a genuine letter between two real people, John Donne the poet and his friend Christopher Brooke, and the storm is not entirely literary because it has some basis (however slim) in Donne's experience on the 1597 Islands Expedition. Therefore, the speaker of the poem (poet-epistoler-adventurer) is a conduit for the self-expression of the real John Donne. The central line of the poem (and others) situates an affective self-portrait of Donne the poet amidst the chaos of the storm.

"The Calme" devotes itself to the elaboration of this debilitating chaos now within the main character. In the last section of "The Calme" (lines 39–56), the speaker struggles to reduce the suffocating confusion and futility he feels to order. He vainly tries to insert some distance between himself and the experience, but the experience has overcome him, and therefore his searching syntax is repeatedly turned back and against itself by the paradoxes now infiltrating him:

> Whether a rotten state, and hope of gaine,
> Or to disuse mee from the queasie paine
> Of being belov'd, and loving, or the thirst
> Of honour, or faire death, out pusht mee first,
> I lose my end: for here as well as I
> A desperate may live, and a coward die.
>
> (39–44)

There is no calm to be found in experience, language in its honesty fails even to produce a façade of control, and the appropriate generic end to the poem has absented itself along with the addressee. In every sense the speaker says: "I lose my end." With great skill the poem stalls, like a ship becalmed, reflecting the transfixed nature of the poet's psyche (55–56).

Donne's strategy of locating a poignant self-portrait within the fictive physical and psychic field of his *istoria* is not unique; it is, in fact, a powerful early-Mannerist topos that reveals much about the psychic impact of the philosophical paradigm-shift being experienced by the early moderns. Both Donne, and Jacopo Pontormo (to instance one of the most stylistically relevant of the Italian cinquecento painters) in his famous *Deposition*, situate a self-representation in anguish within the drama of a specific historical event, the meaning of which is profoundly disturbing and psychically crippling. It is an experience with universal import that threatens to crush the humanity of the artist, a humanity that—as the self-portrait's gaze or address towards the audience of the artwork asserts—we also share. It is the investment of deep emotional resonance throughout a fabric of explicit artifice, the disturbing resonance often rupturing the coherency of that fabric, that assigns an artwork to *early* Mannerism. Donne's diptych miniature history is really a history that becomes a skeptical miniature self-portrait, and not just a portrait of him but also, by extension, of his reader.

If the narrative story of the poem leads back to its writer, so does the relentless projection of artifice. For, quite simply, the artistic overload of the poem makes it a metonymy for the skilful poet. The resultant stereoscopic image of the poet is surprisingly credible: here is a man dismayed by the intensity of his own skeptical perception of reality and yet also of great competence in intellectual and poetic abilities. The balance is beautifully achieved and, in the context of complimentary friendship verse, the latter enables and expresses the former while also acting as something of a dam-wall against its threatening despair. In this way, in their intellectual and emotive acuteness and poetic confidence the verse epistles may well be, in the end, letters of friendship and encouragement not to another, but to oneself: "Thou which art I" ("The Storme," line 1).

The intense skepticism of "The Storme" and "The Calme" is not maintained in the rest of the verse epistles. There is, in general, a retreat from the indecorously disturbing (though not always its complete abandonment) and a motion towards, particularly in the shorter epistles, a sheer embodiment of grace and style (*maniera*). With the disruptive and confronting aspects of skepticism toned down or removed, what remains is a series of poems designed largely, many purely, as effortless and novel displays of art. Many have very little or no substantial content base aside from their own artfulness, and this is as much a fact of their nature as it is a major catalyst for the wonder they elicit. In this way the functioning of Donne's verse epistles is not dissimilar to the functioning of a Mannerist drawing. It is only a sketch, a mere "nothing," and yet how intricate and self-conscious, how perfect in invention and with such adorable grace. It is recognized as an effusion of genius, a rich and complex wine, the taste of which will win over the palate of the discerning consumer. The given drawing, as with the sent verse epistle, is a bequeathal of *difficultà*, an emanance of *virtù*: it is a currency of friendship or social power or dependency paid in the coin of artistic virtuosity.

Aretino claims to preserve a letter from Michelangelo in a golden chalice and craves a mere scrap of a sketch that the master would otherwise throw out so as to live and die with it.[10] The artfulness, undecidable hyperbole, and possible irony of Aretino's remarks further his relevance here. For Donne's exquisitely artful letters to his male friends have him longing similarly. He tells "T. W" in "All haile sweet Poët," "how good it were to see / A Poëm in thy praise, and writ by thee" (23–24). In fact, any letter from Woodward will do, so Donne may imitate its perfect style (29–32). In another poem to "T. W.," "Pregnant again with th'old twins Hope, and Feare," Donne represents himself as a starving beggar all but dead waiting for a letter from Woodward:

> And now thine Almes is given, thy letter'is read,
> The body risen againe, the which was dead,
> And thy poore starveling bountifully fed.
>
> (7–9)

In Donne's letters to his male friends, he regularly condemns his own "harsh verse" and "slimy rimes" with consummate artistry and spells out his devotion to his friend with displays of brilliant poetic virtuosity. To his male friends it is an evidence of friendship; to the great ladies it is a demonstration of professional talent. Both recipient groups are delighted by the wit and skill. The verse epistles to Wotton and Goodyere, and particularly those to the countesses of Huntington and Bedford and the one to Carey and Riche, are more extended showpieces in which poetic invention governs form and length, though more serious issues such as the court, town, and country debate; virtue; and knowing oneself are addressed as well. They are, however, as with the shorter epistles, still showpieces that continue stanza after stanza only as long as Donne is prepared to extend them—and himself.[11]

The "Letter to the Lady *Carey*, and Mrs *Essex Riche*, From *Amyens*" is particularly witty in its solution to the problem of equal superlative praise to two addressees. The poem concludes with the conceit of its being a short gallery with mirrors "at the end" so as "to present the roome twice to our eyes" (55–57). In other words, Donne solves two difficulties, aesthetic and social, in a single flourish at the end. The recipient-reader (whichever of them it might be) is sent back through this poem of praise with the command to regard it as now about herself (if she had not on the first reading), while the coterie reader also wanders the gallery of the poem again astonished at the fresh invention of the final conceit that sent him back to appreciate again what is now an explicitly self-conscious artifact.

The elegies—particularly such fantastic encrustations of wit as "The Bracelet" (XI), "The Comparison" (VIII), "Loves Warre" (XX), "Change" (III) and "The Anagram" (II)—share this mode of showing art but, while still polished, they speak in a more rebellious, sexualized, and anti-*mores* voice appropriate to their neo-Ovidian genre.[12] Another difference is that the majority of the elegies, unlike the verse epistles, though appropriate to the Ovidian elegeic heritage, are relentlessly focused on the physical, sexualized, and female body, though there are a number of male (self-)portraits throughout the collection. Either way, it is relevant that for the Mannerist painter the multivaried representation of the human body is the locus of the most accomplished expressions of *difficultà* and *maniera*. England was extremely slow to recognize the aesthetics of the nude, but some English artists with continental experience distinguish themselves from their compatriots by developing this mode after Italian, French, and Dutch models. Oliver's astonishing drawings, *Nymphs and Satyrs*, *Unidentified Composition with Nude Figures*, *Antiope* (all circa post-1610), and *The Entombment* (post-1596) present to England a strikingly confident portfolio displaying the continental aesthetics of the nude. In 1616 Donne was to sit for Oliver, and it is clear from many passing references in his sermons that his understanding of the visual arts goes beyond the superficial.[13] He observes:

> A picture without any drapery, any clothes about it . . . is much a harder thing, and there is much more art showed in making a naked picture, then in all the rich attire that can be put upon it. (*Sermons*, 8.285)

Here Donne reveals his awareness of the Mannerist obsession with "showing art" and the central role of the nude in this project. The represented body participates in the narrative of the artifact but, more importantly, its formal qualities constitute the very vibration of the voice of the artist, his manner, which at its best merges with that absolute, Mannerist aesthetic criterion, *bella maniera*. The effortlessly and gracefully manipulated, visually represented body speaks the skill of the artist. Flaws in the facility of the *invenzione* of the body constitute an uncertain trembling or an unstylish affectation in the artist's voice. Oliver is as aware of these aesthetic rules as Michelangelo or Bronzino.

Many of Donne's elegies may be approached from this reference point. They stand as little "histories" comprising human figures. The human figures are constructed entirely in order to show much art. As with Oliver's drawings, the primary body via which the male artist speaks is female, and it is usually arranged and rearranged for the scopophilic pleasure of an implied male appreciator. The reverse is true, of course, of the male self-portraits found in "His Picture" (V) and "On his Mistris" (XVI) (to exclude the many more minor and negative male portraits scattered through the elegies), which are thoroughly infused with culturally determined indicators of heterosexually desirable masculinity: a male reader is still implied but he may self-gratifyingly identify with the poet's self-portraits and assume the role of the woman's object of desire. In these cases, instead of delighting in watching the woman's body, the man is narcissistically observing idealized images of himself at the same time as basking in the woman's desire these images supposedly arouse.

In some of the elegies (at one end of the scale), such as "The Anagram," "The Comparison," and "To his Mistress Going to Bed" (XIX), the ostensible narrative figures before us, chiefly the female body, are so overdetermined as to be all but obscured by the artfulness of their form. The voice of the artist overspeaks his apparent subject to the degree that the *istoria* is less self-expressive of its own fiction than a pure metonymy for the *ingenium* of the artist, an *ingenium* that is not merely aesthetic but thoroughly socio-aesthetic. The more dramatic elegies (at the other end of the scale) such as "Jealosie" (I), "Natures lay Ideot" (VII), "The Perfume" (IV), and "On his Mistris" are also exceedingly artfully constructed and also culturally predetermined, but their subject-narrative still manages to remain a major feature.

Ovid, to be sure, is self-conscious, but what makes Donne's elegies

Mannerist is not just the sophisticated recycling of a sophisticated prototype but also the ingenious *horror vacui* of these poems. In "The Perfume" and "On his Mistris," for example, there is the characteristically Mannerist "fear of plain space" resulting in not simply a procession of characters one upon another but a dense crowding of literary tropes and figures. "The Anagram," "The Comparison," "The Bracelet," and "To his Mistress Going to Bed," though containing fewer participating characters, exhibit a similarly intense rhetorical crowding. In all cases, single tenors are regularly overloaded with multiple vehicles. The obsessively foregrounded female body becomes, paradoxically, almost an absence, a pure locus defined not by its own essential nature (something always already absent in Donne's verse) so much as the innumerable shows of *ingenium* jostling within its outline.[14] By analogy, not only does Oliver crowd the space of his *Nymphs and Satyrs* and the *Lamentation over the Dead Christ* with many human figures, but each body is so artfully posed that it contains many displays of grace and style. My analogy here relies on a pun on the word "figure" that is at least as old as Cicero and Quintilian and is repeated in English Renaissance rhetorical and poetical manuals as well as Renaissance art treatises that address the question of the sister arts.

Quintilian's primary metaphor for discussion of language is the body. His starting point is that every word has a figure, a literal Latin inflectional or declined form, and every thought is expressed via language in a particular form just as bodies have particular shapes. Such forms must be varied to avoid monotony of case, tense, foot, sound, structure, and rhythm. Form may be varied on a metaphoric level as well. A schema refers to "a rational change in meaning or language from the ordinary and simple form, that is to say, a change analogous to that involved by sitting, lying down on something or looking back." Tropes, figures, and schemas refer to a poetic or rhetorical alteration in language "given by art." Thus, language presents itself like an artificially (re-)arrangeable and displayed body. Quintilian goes on to specify, as Cicero did, what form of body language should take for diverse purposes. Some forms are to be more artificial than others, such as epideictic, but it is always conceded that poets have more licence in this regard than orators.[15]

Even for a poet, Donne goes well beyond classical decorum in his use of figures. Analogous to the Mannerist painters, Donne's elegeic bodies are rich sites of artifice, as is the very fabric of their expression. His manner always drives his subjects away from *natura* and further into the realm of *artificio*. The success of his manner ("style" in its relative definition), dependent upon invention, technical accomplishment, grace and facility, sees it merge with the aesthetic ideal of *bella maniera* ("style" in its absolute sense according to the mannerist definition of high artifice and grace). In the process it becomes apparent that, while for Quintilian language is bodily, for Donne bodies are no more nor less than language. "The Anagram" states this theory explictly:

> Though all her parts be not in th'usual place,
> She'hath yet an Anagram of a good face.
> If we might put the letters but one way,
> In the lean dearth of words, what could wee say?
>
> (15–18)

Quite. And this is not just relevant to the ugly hag topos but is generally applicable to Donne's modus operandi in the elegies. The represented (usually female) body is whatever he chooses whenever he chooses, is always effortlessly modeled and is always the literary incarnation of his *ingenium*. "To his Mistress Going to Bed" demonstrates this point plainly, while "Natures lay Ideot" demonstrates it via witty analogy. The represented body serves not itself but the artist. It is his self-expression according to the canon of high artfulness, effortless invention, the *difficultà:facilità* formula. This Mannerist emphasis on the *virtù* of the artist harmonizes with key generic traits of the English elegy of the 1590s, chiefly its expression of youthful, fashionably rebellious male power and desire defined against a female other. The sophisticated control, manipulation, overwriting, and even need of the female body is fully socio-aesthetic.

The Mannerists strain the definition of decorum itself by raising the acceptable level of artificiality, a raising of the stakes that problematizes such key art terms as mimesis and grace. For Donne, the pursuit of writing the self-portrait of his *ingenium* on paper is a self-conscious project that necessarily produces an exponential flourishing of literary and rhetorical artifice. Nothing is stable or immutable and nothing is single, for his mind is not static, and the thrill for him as well as for the reader is in his ability to maintain both the pace (a sign of effortlessness) and yet also some coherent rationality (a sign of control) within what is a careering verbal excess. The result is a demonstration of sheer artistic *virtù*. At times the artifice runs ahead of the subject, and further artifice is immediately required to tie it back to the subject in hand lest the entire artifact explode apart in an anarchy of invention. The mannerist artefact is regularly poised at this point of aesthetic risk. A version of this moment occurs in this passage of "Loves Warre":

> To mew me in a Ship, is to inthrall
> Mee in a prison, that weare like to fall;
> Or in a Cloyster, save that there men dwell
> In a calme heaven, here in a swaggering hell.
> Long voyages are long consumptions,
> And ships are carts for executions.
> Yea they are Deaths; Is't not all one to flye
> Into an other World, as t'is to dye?
>
> (21–28)

Here the speaker's experience of sea voyage as volunteer-adventurer is presented negatively via a list of likenesses: it is imprisonment in a prison "that weare like to fall," dwelling in a swaggering hell, a long consumption, a cart for execution, travel to the new world, and even death itself. Here is the *invenzione* of *horror vacui*: one thing becomes all things in an effortless supply. However, such overdetermination also throws up the point of greatest aesthetic risk and therefore the moment of greatest potential for display of artistic skill. Enthralled in a cloister? The "cloyster" is the metaphor that is not. It is suggested, presumably, by the idea of isolation in a cabin, but is immediately suggestive of the wrong tone and must be redeemed by its transformation from metaphor to antithesis. The generation and reinclusion of the contextually unexpected image rely on the speaker's ingenuity. He does not blot his paper, his discourse can co-opt all, like and unlike, to the purpose in hand—because really, the purpose in hand is effortless co-option itself. An aesthetic difficulty is raised only to be overcome with facility.

I will close these general remarks on the elegies with a more detailed discussion of "On his Mistris" (XVI), particularly in terms of its exploitation of multiple resources of meaning for the term "invention." Poetically speaking, "On his Mistris" is "a delectable poeme" grounded on "some fine inuention" as Gascoigne advises.[16] The "fine inuention" structuring its *istoria* is really an imaginative projection of the mind of the poet-speaker as he argues that his mistress remain home while he travels abroad. Each major component of the artifact—including the oath with which it commences (1–12), the hypothetical characters and behaviors that form its story (13–56) and, to consider the end of the story also as a distinct component in itself, the striking dream that concludes the poem (50–56)—each of these components is constructed and elaborated with consummate artistic skill. The oath manifests the characteristic interest of the Mannerist aesthetic in prolixity in small compass as it burgeons with no sign of strain. Even an oath, a passing expletive, elaborates into a sign of endless and effortless supply: it is a clever show of artifice. The characters of the *istoria*, the imagined Frenchmen, Italians, Dutch, the mistress herself, and the speaker himself, are similarly sites of artistry, of *invenzione*. Further, the *istoria* is doubly a fiction: it is in total the product of Donne's *ingenium*, but it is also the product of the speaker's *ingenium* for the events it describes do not actually occur fictively; they are purely the fictive speaker's argument.

As an argument, the poem functions as a form of deliberative oration, and invention in it may be defined rhetorically as "the discovery of valid or seemingly valid arguments to render one's cause plausible."[17] Thomas Wilson, following Cicero (*De orat.* 1.142–43) sums up thus: "For whereas invention helpeth to find matter, and disposition serveth to place arguments, elocution getteth words to set forth invention and with such beauty commendeth the matter that reason seemeth to be clad in purple, walking afore both bare and naked."[18] The sites of artistic *invenzione* function simultaneously as the invented arguments of oratory, they are the reasons why his mistress should necessarily stay home as well as the displays of the poet's artistic skill. In this way, strictly speaking, artistic *invenzione* is also oratorical elocution, and possibly more particularly Wilson's exornation. Donne more or less follows Wilson's seven-part orational form with some major restructuring. He begins with an elaborate "entrance" (1–12) to gain the attention and ear of the judge (simultaneously the fictive speaker's mistress and Donne's coterie audience of aesthetic judges). He combines the "narration" and "proposition" in a short statement of the matter (13–18) and omits entirely the statement of the "division." In the "confirmation" he argues with an example (Boreas and Orithea) that not even his mistress' beauty can render the wind and sea secure and thus her travel is an unnecessary tempting of fate (19–25) and that she may instead enjoy the spiritual union of separated lovers (25–26)—this last point made with a knowing nod ("this flattery") to his coterie readers. The bulk of the poem is the "confutation," the "dissolving or wiping-away" to quote Wilson[19], of her counter-argument that she may go disguised (27–43). This is executed with much art and many examples and it is followed by examples of how she may spend her time at home awaiting him (43–56). Dispensing with a regular "conclusion," he chooses to end on a stunning display of *enargeia* (50–56) so that his mistress-judge (who becomes the subject at this point) will not only see his reasoning but feel the emotive force of his persuasion; and so that Donne's coterie audience (his aesthetic judges) will receive a final impression of the astounding poetic skill of Donne as artist.[20]

Wilson notes how the deliberative oration may persuade or dissuade,[21] but Donne, in a show of art, demonstrates how it may perform both functions at the same time. Rhetorically, the poem operates within its fictive scenario to dissuade the mistress from "love by wayes so dangerous" (12). The strength of the opening oath conspires with the intensity of the various character portraits to argue in the strongest terms against her accompanying him. However, viewed aesthetically, and in the context of the poet-Donne writing for his coterie audience, the oath by its form and content suggests that this poem, this display of oratorical and poetical skill, will surpass all that has gone before, and the following artful characters, as sites of *invenzione*, only prove the superior skill of the poet. The wit, *invenzione*, and effortless facility of the elegy persuade the reader of Donne's poetic power. The deliberative oration functions in dissuading the mistress to persuade the reader. The impact of the invention of arguments is for her chiefly oratorical, and for the reader initially aesthetic but ultimately also rhetorical. And the confirmation of this dual conquest comes in the superb ending.

At the end the speaker urges his mistress to "dreame me some happinesse" not to "fright thy Nurse"

> With midnights startings, crying out, oh, oh
> Nurse, ô my love is slaine, I saw him goe
> O'r the white Alpes alone; I saw him I,
> Assail'd, fight, taken, stabb'd, bleed, fall, and die.
> Augure me better chance, except dread *Jove*
> Thinke it enough for me, to'have had thy love.

(51–56)

Presumably an ending such as this is designed to give graphic and emotive charge to the pervasive theme that travel is fraught with danger and thus is no exercise for a woman. Thus, it stands as a powerful end to a deliberative oration employing to perfection the visual and emotive force of Ciceronian *enargeia*. It is here that the peak of oratorical persuasion simultaneously dissuades the mistress (from attending the speaker) and persuades the reader (of Donne's artistic *virtù*).

In this section, Donne creates an example of *enargeia* directly out of Quintilian's theory of it in the *Institutio oratoria*. Quintilian notes how the mind when unoccupied or absorbed by daydreams is haunted by visions of such vividness that among other things "we imagine we are travelling abroad, crossing the sea, fighting"; we believe at the time we are not dreaming but simply doing. Now, if the orator is to effect the same vividness and emotive pull as these visions he must construct all that might be imagined to go with a situation. Quintilian's example is that of a man being murdered:

> Shall I not see the assassin burst suddenly from his hiding-place, the victim tremble, cry for help, beg for mercy, or turn to run? Shall I not see the fatal blow delivered and the stricken body fall? Will not the blood, the deathly pallor, the groan of agony, the death-rattle, be indelibly impressed upon my mind? (6.2.31)

The objective of all this, says Quintilian, is to transmit the experience described with the utmost force to one's auditors. The speaker must speak from the position of the one he describes and feel what he describes as if it were he himself. This strategy of *enargeia* makes the performance all the more forceful, affectively involving the auditors. Donne utilizes Quintilian's example of the murdered man, recontextualizes it into his own fiction, and enacts Quintilian's theory in this elegy with great effectiveness.

A significant modification of Quintilian's arrangement is that Donne puts the described experience into the mind and words of his mistress (merging Quintilian's sourcing of the idea in dreams with his demonstration of it in oratorical practice). This relocation of the experience to a second person rather than the subject himself serves a particular purpose that returns us to the social context. Donne's speaker is reaffirming his mistress' dependency upon him. This closing passage implants in her a way of thinking. It guarantees her dependence upon him while he travels by constructing her as a devoted mistress with no independence (thereby solving the problem raised in "Natures lay Ideot"). The passage is an example for her in his absence: while he travels and acts in the world she, remaining at home unoccupied, is to be filled with not simply images of him but with experiences of her utter and childlike dependence upon him. This is reinforced by fears of his death. Thus, he may travel the world in freedom, knowing that she is "safe" at home, safe in terms of a possession well guarded. She is guarded doubly: by not being subject to the lecherous world's scrutiny and by herself only seeing images of him and her need for him. The deliberative oration is thorough, dissuading her from others' view and persuading her to view only the speaker. She will be no one's object of desire but his and she will have no object of desire but him. She has been located and defined by the politics of the male gaze: it precisely transfixes her but leaves him wholly free.

The force of the culturally loaded *enargeia* also serves to absorb the male readers into the Donnean fantasy. The cultural paradigm affirmed here is palatable to and functional for the male readers. However, the chaining of the mistress to the speaker, the presentation of himself as desirable tragic hero and the ambivalent nobility of his love for her in the concluding couplet together betray his need for her utter devotion to him. What this reveals, of course, is that the speaker's dependence upon his mistress' devotion and affirmation is as real as Donne's dependence upon his readers' devotion and affirmation. Their devotion to and affirmation of both Donne himself and their own selves as a group is reified via the communally acknowledged display of poetic artifice saturated with shared cultural assumptions. The fulfilment of this need for affirmation, a need equally present in the verse epistles, is induced in the only way Donne can be sure he will succeed, via the interactive, socio-aesthetic cycle of the *difficultà:facilità* formula. Showing art is surely the showing of oneself, but the self that speaks in a parade of competence through these self-confirming fictions is simultaneously more and less than it seems.

NOTES

1. My quotations from Donne's verse come from *The Complete English Poems of John Donne*, ed. C. A. Patrides (London: Dent, 1985).
2. This is not to deny the existence of three facts: continental limning, a (less than resoundingly coherent) large-scale tradition in England, and "story-work" in miniature.

3. On this see John Shearman, *Mannerism* (1967; rpt. Harmondsworth: Penguin, 1977), 21–22; David Summers, *Michelangelo and the Language of Art* (Princeton: Princeton University Press, 1981), 89–90, 177–84.

4. *The Sermons of John Donne*, 10 vols., ed. George R. Potter and Evelyn M. Simpson (Berkeley and Los Angeles: University of California Press, 1953–62), 4.183–84.

5. From *A Cypress Grove* (1619, 1623). *Drummond of Hawthornden: Poems and Prose* ed. Robert H. Macdonald (Edinburgh: Scottish Academic Press, 1976), 154.

6. See Clayton D. Lein, "Donne's 'The Storme': The Poem and the Tradition," *English Literary Renaissance* 4 (1974): 137–63.

7. A. C. Partridge, *John Donne: Language and Style* (London: André Deutsch, 1978), 51; George Puttenham, *The Arte of English Poesie* ed. Gladys Doidge Willcock and Alice Walker (1936; rpt. Cambridge: Cambridge University Press, 1970), 239; Cicero, *Orator* 37–39, 42; Aristotle, *Rhet.* 1.3, 3.12.

8. Oliver's narrative drawings are reproduced in Roy Strong, *The English Renaissance Miniature* (1983; rev. ed., London: Thames and Hudson, 1984), 145, 148–49.

9. The extracts in *John Donne: The Critical Heritage*, ed. A. J. Smith (1975; rpt. London: Routledge and Kegan Paul, 1985) make clear Donne's involvement in this system. From "The Storme," the "*Hilliard* drawne" passage is particularly popular (84–85, 131, 136, 57); as is the "Another *Fiat*" couplet (33, 34). Sections from "The Calme" are also well-regarded, with Jonson learning the "Feathers and dust" passage by heart and echoing line 14 in *The New Inn*, 69, 44–45. The quotation and recontextualization of masterful artists' novel and brilliantly executed *difficultà* is a mannerist trademark.

10. *Aretino: Selected Letters*, trans. George Bull (Harmondsworth: Penguin, 1976), 237–38.

11. On their artfulness see *John Donne: The Satires, Epigrams and Verse Letters*, ed. W. Milgate (Oxford: Clarendon, 1967), xxxviii–xxxix; Margaret Maurer, "The Real Presence of Lucy Russell, Countess of Bedford, and the Terms of John Donne's 'Honour is so Sublime Perfection,' " *English Literary History* 47 (1980): 205–34; and Barbara L. DeStefano, "Evolution of Extravagant Praise in Donne's Verse Epistles," *Studies in Philology* 81 (1984): 75–93.

12. I note here two studies of the elegies I have found particularly useful: Arthur F. Marotti, *John Donne, Coterie Poet* (Madison: University of Wisconsin Press, 1986), 44–66; and Stanley Fish, "Masculine Persuasive Force: Donne and Verbal Power," in *Soliciting Interpretation: Literary Theory and Seventeenth-Century English Poetry*, ed. Elizabeth D. Harvey and Katharine Eisaman Maus (Chicago: University of Chicago Press, 1990), 223–52.

13. I demonstrate this in greater detail in my book, *The English Mannerist Poets and the Visual Arts* (Madison, NJ: Fairleigh Dickinson University Press, 1998): the elegies are not discussed in it. Oliver's works just referred to are reproduced in Strong, *English Renaissance Miniature*, 148–49; and Lindsay Stainton and Christopher White, *Drawing in England From Hilliard to Hogarth* (London: British Museum Publications, 1987), 49–51.

14. Arcimboldo's portraits show how the form of a subject may absent itself as a diversity of artistic ingenuity explodes from within. The one is truly the many, and the subject speaks only the artistic *virtù* of the portraitist. Rosso's mask designs function similarly (*Mannerism*, 153).

15. Quintilian, *Institutio oratoria*, trans. H. E. Butler (1920; rpt. London: Heinemann, 1960), 9.1.11–14; 10.1.28. Cf. Cicero, *De orat.* 1.70; *Orator* 37, 42, 66–68, 201–2.

16. *Elizabethan Critical Essays,* 2 vols., ed. G. Gregory Smith (1904; rpt. Oxford: Oxford University Press, 1964), 1.47.

17. Cicero, *De inventione,* trans. H. M. Hubbell (1949; rpt. London: Heinemann, 1968), 1.9. Puttenham allows that the poet is often "an oratour, or perswader" (233; cf. 240).

18. Thomas Wilson, *The Art of Rhetoric* (1560), ed. Peter E. Medine (University Park: Pennsylvania State University Press, 1994), 187.

19. Wilson, *The Art of Rhetoric,* 51.

20. Mannerist painting may profitably be discussed along these lines as deliberative oration.

21. Wilson, *The Art of Rhetoric,* 70.

Donne's Elegies and the Ugly Beauty Tradition

HEATHER DUBROW

"THE AUTUMNALL," "THE ANAGRAM," AND "THE COMPARISON" ARE IN SOME respects catalogues of the characteristics of the ugly beauty tradition, even though the third poem deviates significantly from it in not actually praising its unappetizing heroine. The cultural pressures behind that tradition, especially anxieties about gender and mutability, are strikingly prominent in Donne's texts. The rhetorical strategies most typical of ugly beauty poems also recur throughout these three poems: we find many examples of antitheses, of their erosion, of equivocations, and above all of threats. Here, as elsewhere in his canon, Donne typically responds to receiving threats by issuing them. This maneuver is the global speech act around which "The Curse" is organized, the direct speech act on which "Womans Constancy" culminates, an indirect speech act in poems ranging from "Satyre I" to "The Message"—but nowhere are threats more significant than in Donne's poems about so-called ugly beauties. Despite these and other similarities, however, Donne's elegies also diverge from the ugly beauty tradition in the emphasis on male rivalry that is latent in "The Anagram" and explicit, even emphatic, in "The Comparison." Thus, these texts help us further to understand both the conventions in question and Donne's own status as resident alien in the discourse of Petrarchism.

Written to an aging woman generally assumed to be Magdalen Herbert,[1] "The Autumnall" has received a little more critical attention than most of its author's so-called minor poems. Yet many of its oddities remain in need of explication: troubling issues such as his description of "Winter-faces" (37) in a poem ostensibly devoted to flattery have not been fully explored. Though the praise of the beauty of mature women had classical precedents, including an epigram in the Greek Anthology,[2] Donne's approach to that subject, like his approach to the ugly beauty tradition as a whole, remains idiosyncratic and unsettling.

Opening on the declaration, "No *Spring*, nor *Summer* Beauty hath such grace, / As I have seen in one *Autumn all* face" (1–2), the poem allies itself with other members of the ugly beauty tradition in its emphasis on comparisons and contrasts. Donne proceeds to describe the appealing moderation of his subject's attractions ("This is her tolerable Tropique clyme" [10]), thus demonstrating that, for all its tensions, the poem represents a warm and urbane tribute on one important level. He is, however, also at pains to rule out of court—and therefore to introduce into the courtroom—alternative modes of description and alternative types of women with whom his lady might be confused: "Call not these wrinkles, graves" (13), or "But name not Winterfaces, whose skin's slacke; / Lanke, as an unthrifts purse; but a soules sacke" (37–38). Ending on the promise, "I shall ebbe on with them, who home-ward goe" (50), he identifies his state with that of autumnal beauties, thus anticipating more disturbing identifications between men and their mistresses in "The Comparison."

On one level, then, "The Autumnall" exemplifies distancing devices used by Sidney and other writers in the tradition: in the course of distinguishing his subject from younger, more conventionally attractive women, Donne differentiates himself from the poets, Petrarchan and otherwise, who praise them. But at the same time, this poem, like others by Donne, is concerned not merely with distance but also with edges, margins, or brinks. The lady is repeatedly constructed as between other states. She is positioned chronologically between the spring and summer to which line one refers and the winter mentioned in line 37, just as the description of her is structurally located within the poem itself between those points. Similarly, "Here, where still Evening is; not noone, nor night" (21) paradoxically associates her with the peacefulness of evening (a peacefulness intensified if, responding to Donne's pun, one reads "still" adverbially) and yet reminds us of the time of day that evening follows and, more to the point, the period that will shortly ensue. Once again the subject of the poem mimes the text itself, for "The Autumnall" locates itself on the margins of bitterness and satire without ever crossing over into them.

Its own position on the verge stems from Donne's attempts, largely successful, to control a series of anxieties and threats. Like other poets in the tradition, he is clearly preoccupied with the fear of the loss of beauty. And, not surprisingly, he is preoccupied with the fear of the loss of life: though the poem seemingly addresses itself to autumn, its references to graves, resurrection, and "living Deaths-heads" (43) suggest that it is really more concerned with winter, with death itself. The text, after all, concludes on an allusion to the poet's own demise, reminding us of Cathy Yandell's observation that in French Renaissance poems, the carpe diem tradition may encode the poet's fears of his own mortality.[3]

Donne tries to control these and other fears through his usual linguistic games:

> If we love thing long sought, Age is a thing
> Which we are fifty yeares in compassing.
> If transitory things, which soone decay,
> Age must be lovelyest at the latest day.
>
> (33–36)

The playfulness of these compressed syllogisms as well as the lack of firmness behind the if/then formula in effect bracket these statements. Above all, though, Donne protects the subject of his poem—and his own claim to be bestowing praise rather than drawing on the satiric potentialities of the epistle—through the kind of diacritical maneuver he performs in all three poems. That is, not only is the lady distinguished from younger beauties and his poem distinguished from the more conventional lyrics, Petrarchan and otherwise, that praise them, but he also repeatedly differentiates the subject of the lyric from the less attractive women with whom she might be confused—and whom she will in time become. Thus "name not *Winter-faces*" (37) reminds us that they could be named and that an honest poem addressed to this same woman some years later might well feel compelled to name them. Here, as in the phrase "Call not these wrinkles, *graves*" (13), the emphasis on the speech acts of naming and calling reminds us that the poet himself is engaged in such acts, with his ability to name and call, rather than any objective assessment, determining how this autumnal beauty is viewed. In these lines, so reminiscent of similar strategies elsewhere in the ugly beauty tradition, Donne at once expresses and contains anxieties that an autumnal beauty is in fact, or will shortly become, wintry—and does so by drawing attention to his own ability to construct that beauty as he pleases.

"The Anagram" is based on several sources, most notably Berni and Tasso.[4] Like Donne's two other ugly beauty poems, it also plays on the paradox, a form that clearly interested Donne. Building on such precedents and models, he declares that Flavia merely reverses the usual criteria for beauty: "though her eyes be small, her mouth is great" (3). But for the monochromatic mood that characterizes some other poems in the ugly beauty tradition, such as Sidney's sonnet on Mopsa, Donne substitutes a startling, unsettling range of emotions and tonalities. We move from obvious, even crude mockery ("Give her thine, and she hath a maydenhead"[8]) to a melancholy meditation on the loss, actual or feared, of beauty (" 'Tis lesse griefe to be foule, then to' have beene faire" [32]) to a down-to-earth assessment of the advantages of not being attractive ("in long journeyes, cloth, and leather use" [34]) and back to crude jokes ("Whom Dildoes, Bed-staves, and her Velvet Glasse / Would be as loath to touch as Joseph was" [53–54]). The final quotation, incidentally, refers to the loyal Joseph's refusal to be seduced by his master Potiphar's wife, a story told in Genesis 39, and thus introduces yet another transgressive woman into a poem, the male author of which is engaged in transgressing against epideictic norms.

The range of tone in "The Anagram" stems from the range of agendas Donne pursues. As always, one should not neglect the element of play; Donne, whose own verse delights in reversals and puzzles, constructs a woman who is herself an anagram. Thus, once again, the poet's verse and the woman it describes are allied; and once again the light-hearted hint of that similarity gestures towards deeper and more troubling elisions of gender, which remain subterranean here but emerge in full force in "The Comparison." But if playful wit is one impetus behind "The Anagram," the author of the "The Autumnall" and the *Devotions* is, predicatably, impelled as well by the fear of mutability and its vice-regent disease that so often drives the ugly beauty tradition. As he observes within this poem, "Love built on beauty, soone as beauty, dies, / Chuse this face, chang'd by no deformities" (27–28). In expressing these anxieties about deformity, he wittily deforms a trope associated with Petrarchism in particular and with Elizabethan love poetry in general:

> Women are all like Angels; the faire be
> Like those which fell to worse; but such as shee,
> Like to good Angels, nothing can impaire.
>
> (29–31)

Thus, the genuinely angelic women of conventional love poetry become fallen angels, whereas Donne's foul angel becomes a good one,

and the boundaries between normative women and their transgressive sisters are again called into question, though in the less threatening
guise of a game.

The poem is impelled by anxieties about both literal disease and
decay and the moral decay that Donne genders female. Marrying a
foul woman, he explains, ensures a faithful wife. In making this argument, Donne reveals a section of the genetic code of this literary type
more clearly than do any of the poems studied earlier. The fear of infidelity is at the roots of a general misogyny that, as Donne's love lyrics suggest, encompasses women in general; the ugly beauty tradition
allows Donne at once to express that misogyny and to localize it by
attacking one, presumably fictive, woman. He thus transmutes a potential defensiveness in the face of the mutability associated with
Dame Nature and the infidelity associated with earthly women into a
posture that is once again offensive in both senses. In so doing, Donne
indulges and denies his hostility, a pattern we have encountered in his
epistles to noblewomen and in ugly beauty poems by other writers.

But this elegy differs from its counterparts in the tradition in one
important respect. "Marry, and love thy *Flavia*," Donne declares in
the first line of the lyric, through his pronoun associating the woman
with a male addressee, the shadowy figure that we are permitted to
forget for much of the poem. He reemerges, however, in a few lines,
notably "Oh what a soveraigne Plaister will shee bee, / If thy past
sinnes have taught thee jealouise" (37–38). To interpret the presence
of this male figure we need to turn to "The Comparison," in which his
equivalent is not an extra with a walk-on part but a central character.

"The Comparison" is in many ways the most interesting of Donne's
three poems in the ugly beauty tradition. Written by a poet who often
genders duplicity female, it opens by establishing a complex and perhaps even duplicitous relationship to literary tradition. It twists Petrarchan tropes; and it appears to be a familiar version of the ugly beauty
convention, only to slide into the misogynistic satire that is the road
not taken in that tradition, its dark underside. The elegy begins on an
apparently admiring description of the first woman's pearl-like perspiration:

> As the sweet sweat of Roses in a Still,
> As that from which chaf'd muskats pores doth trill,
> As the Almighty Balme of th'early East,
> Such are the sweat drops on my Mistris breast.

> (1–4)

Thus, the lyric invokes staples of the most conventional love poetry, notably tropes deploying flowers and dawn, to perform the decidedly unconventional task of celebrating perspiration. In so doing, it seemingly positions itself among the type of ugly beauty poems, the tone of which we cannot determine with certainty, such as Carew's tribute to the mole. For the contemporary reader is not completely persuaded by this paean to perspiration, this song of sweat, and I think an early modern reader would also be made uneasy by Donne's hyperboles, even though perspiration was no doubt more acceptable in that culture than in our own. From another perspective, Donne is establishing an uneasy relationship to Petrarchism as well. The reference to pearls at once participates in and mocks that discourse, for whether or not Laura lacks pity, she apparently lacks perspiration glands, even when seen under the midday sun of Italy.

Donne abruptly shifts, however, to a different mode of comparison and a different literary model. For he proceeds to contrast his speaker's lady, perspiring but inspiring, with the indubitably repulsive mistress of that other man. As a result, his poem assumes a version of a chiasmic structure, playing the ideal Petrarchan mistress against the speaker's lady and then that lady against the far from ideal mistress of another man. Thus, Donne also plays two literary forms against each other, the epideictic mode of the ugly beauty tradition versus satire. And thus, he deflects from the speaker's lady onto her ostensible opposite number ambivalent or even negative responses to her perspiration and perhaps indirectly to her other bodily functions as well. The contrast between the two women and between the two literary types dramatizes the poet's bifurcated responses to a single woman or to the construction of woman.[5]

Proceeding to elaborate the contrast between the two women, Donne crams his lyric with a series of images that seem odd even when one considers their author and their roots in that odd convention, the praise of ugly beauty. Each woman is associated with a version of androgyny. First, he plays his mistress's balm against the "spermatique issue of ripe menstrous boiles" (8) produced by the other woman. *Spermatique*, to be sure, could be defined in ways that would not unsettle gender: it might refer to seed in general, which Galen and many later authorities believed that women produce.[6] The *Oxford English Dictionary* assures us that the term may merely mean "generative, productive."[7] These glosses are not, however, unproblematical: whether women produced seed remained debatable during the late sixteenth and seventeenth centuries, and the denotation of *spermatique* as "generative" was rare in that period. The alternative denotation of the adjective, an allusion to male seed in particular, is surely at least latent in the phrase and is activated by the other references in the poem to androgyny. Thus, the line links images of male and female fluids, making gender itself more fluid, a point to which I will return. Moreover, the passage associates the male emission with reproductive vigor, whereas the female counterpart is linked to disease, which again demonstrates the connections between the ugly beauty tradition and a misogyny generated by and expressed through bodily dysfunction.

Donne proceeds to describe the genitals of the apparently attractive woman in equally androgynous terms:

> Then like the Chymicks masculine equall fire,
> Which in the Lymbecks warme wombe doth inspire
> Into th'earths worthless durt a soule of gold,
> Such cherishing heat her best lov'd part doth hold.
>
> (35–38)

Donne's peculiar alchemy of love virtually transforms the woman's "best lov'd part" (38) into the best loved part of a man. The doctrine of sexual homology cannot wholly explain this passage, not least because that doctrine itself neglects the variety and inconsistency of anatomical decriptions in Renaissance medical tracts.[8] Gender is further confounded by a series of pronouns that identifies the unattractive woman with the speaker's male anatonist: "*Thy* head" . . . "*Thine's* like worme eaten trunkes" . . . "*thy* tann'd skins" (19,25,32; emphasis added). While on one level such phrases merely assume the presence of an elided word ("thy mistress' head" and so forth), on another level the referent of the pronouns is the male listener, thus equated with his mistress. (Consistently relying on the third-person pronoun for his speaker's lady, Donne does not identify that pair of lovers with each other in the same way, thereby preserving yet another form of distance.)

If the androgyny of the poem is odd, so too are the seemingly appealing tropes associated with the speaker's mistress. Her head's ideal roundness, we are told, recalls the apple in Eden and the golden apple that inspired the fateful rivalry between Juno, Venus, and Miverva—both tropes that do more to intensify the preoccupation with evil and competitiveness in the poem than to persuade us of the lady's charms. And these ambivalent images culminate in the extraordinary opposition—or apparent opposition—between the experiences of making love to each of these women:

> Are not your kisses then as filthy, 'and more,
> As a worme sucking an invenom'd sore?
> Doth not thy fearefull hand in feeling quake,
> As one which gath'ring flowers, still fear'd a snake?
> Is not your last act harsh, and violent,
> As when a Plough a stony ground doth rent?
> So kisse good Turtles, so devoutly nice
> Are Priests in handling reverent sacrifice,
> And such in searching wounds the Surgeon is
> As wee, when wee embrace, or touch, or kisse.
>
> (43–52)

Notice yet again the emphasis on disease, with its implication that the phallic worm is feeding off a sore that is gendered female.

Why, then, does this poem end on so ambivalent a description of a sexuality that is ostensibly presented positively? Given that the tradition of ugly beauty poems regularly involves so many other forms of antithesis, including an often implicit contrast between the woman in question and a normative beauty, why does Donne add another antithetical pattern, his dramatized conflict between two opposed men? And why does he identify one of those men with the repulsive mistress, in that and other ways eliding gender categories?

Some answers emerge promptly when one recalls the threats previously identified in the ugly beauty tradition and in Donne's own contributions to it; other responses provide a new perspective on that tradition. Most obviously, this poem, like lyrics in praise of ugly beauty, is rooted in concerns about both poetic and more personal rivalries. By establishing a competitive relationship with another male, Donne characteriscally deflects onto that unfortunate lover his antagonisms towards Petrarch and other earlier love poets, thus countering the anxiety of influence. At the same time, this lyric, like other members of its tradition, transforms its male readers from potential rivals, the role in which Donne so often casts other men, into participants in misogynistic jokes. The poem thus rewrites the competitiveness that Donne subdues in his early verse epistles by refocusing a whole series of other tensions on a single male antagonist.

Other threats, of course, involve gender. The pronouns that identify the rival male with his lady clarify a tension latent in other poems in the ugly beauty tradition: these pronouns not only signal but also enact the assumption that a man is judged by the women with whom he is associated to the point where they may virtually be equated: "And like a bunch of ragged carrets stand / The short swolne fingers of *thy* gouty hand" (33–34; emphasis added). Twentieth-century journalists may have invented the term *trophy wife*, but they could have taught Donne and other members of his culture nothing they did not already know about the mirror image of that phenomenon, the denigration of a man because of the unattractive or unfaithful woman with whom he is associated. That denigration is also threatening because it may stage and intensify the broader cultural fear that has recently been studied by many critics: the anxiety that male and female cannot be readily distinguished.[9] Once again the counterdiscourses of English Petrarchism both respond to and replicate the erosion of gender distinctions.

Of course, the lyric draws our attention as well to another tension associated with gender. If other poems in the ugly beauty tradition are grounded in anxieties about the changes that aging and gynecological or obstetrical problems could wreak on the bodies of beautiful women, this one testifies to a different but cognate anxiety. As Swift might have put it, "Can *Chloe*, heavenly *Chloe*, smell?" Donne's elegy "The Perfume" demonstrates his own consciousness of both pleasant and repellent smells, but "The Comparison" also invites speculations about the cultural construction of odor in Tudor and Stuart culture. Perhaps critics have thus far devoted so little attention to the subject because it makes us uneasy: in many academic forums it appears to be more acceptable to discuss sexualities—including one's own—than sweat.

Donne, as we have already seen, again responds to all these tensions through a series of deflections. Misogynistic antagonism towards all women is channeled towards the ugly beauty of this poem; if other poets in the tradition praise such a woman to shelter other women, or their images of them, from comparable attack, Donne renders that pattern explicit by actually juxtaposing two mistresses in the lyric. Similarly, potential rivalries with male companions are deflected onto a single target, the unfortunate lover in the poem, with other men implicitly invited to share in misogynistic jokes. And poetic rivalries are transformed into the rivalry between the two men. In short, like

so many other poets in the ugly beauty tradition, Donne creates a series of diacritical oppositions to distance himself from what threatens
him, whether it be the inanity of conventional Petrarchism, the vulnerability of conventional beauties, or the pugnacity of relationships between men.

Donne's misogynistic antagonism is, then, not suppressed but simply redirected, and its continuing presence helps to explain the extraordinary image of sex on which the poem culminates. I have argued
elsewhere that the reference to the violating priest in the "Epithalamion made at Lincolnes Inne" ("Like an appointed lambe, when
tenderly / The priest comes on his knees t'embowell her" [89–90])
stems from the author's guilt about his own drive to dominate and
violate: in response, he mystifies and sanctifies violence.[10] The same
dynamic impels the contrast between two modes of sexuality at the
conclusion of this poem.

But much as the line between Petrarchism and anti-Petrarchism is
erased in so many other ugly beauty poems, here both that contrast
and several other distinctions break down: the poem undermines the
very diacritical structures it erects. The line between male and female
repeatedly disappears, as I have observed. And while the contrast between the beautiful and repulsive mistresses does not totally disap-
pear, it is certainly blurred. The narrative of the golden apple pivots,
after all, on a beauty contest determined not by the intrinsic loveliness
of the contenders but by the suasiveness of their bribes, a plot that
renders problematical the seemingly objective and clear-cut beauty
contest enacted in this poem. Donne's evocation of this myth is all the
more telling when one recalls how seldom he draws on mythology.[11]
Alerted by its presence and by the adjoining association of the attractive mistress with the Fall, readers may well speculate about whether
lovely and loathsome women can be distinguished as easily as this
poem insists, a question provoked as well by "The Anagram," "The
Autumnall," and many other texts in their tradition. And is the man
who loves and praises the beautiful one really so separate from his
foolish opposite number?[12]

Such questions raise another: is Donne skillfully manipulating these
ironies and contradictions, as literary curators who see poetry as a
well-wrought urn might argue, or is he a victim of them , as those who
see poetry as another shard of a warring culture might maintain? The
first reading would suggest an ironic critique of his speaker, and the
second, entanglement in the problems of the ugly beauty tradition, in

a net whose windows have been sealed. These questions resemble the debate about the purposiveness of the contradictions and confusions in the *Holy Sonnets*.[13] In neither case is the issue a simple one, but in the instance of "The Comparison," Donne's conclusion—"Leave her, and I will leave comparing thus, / She, and comparisons are odious" (53–54)—favors the second interpretive strategy. He is, I suggest, sheltering behind the old proverb about comparisons to reveal his own unease with the divided aims and divided results of his own comparisons. He characteristically concludes the poem by deflecting some of his unease about the subject onto the male rival whom he has attacked all along.

"The Comparison," like "The Autumnall" and "The Anagram," testifies to some of the reasons he found that counterdiscourse singularly congenial. The poet who saw the skeleton beneath the skin—and also saw the viruses beneath it and the perspiration on it, though he would have assigned different names to the former—found a tradition rooted in fears of bodily mutability and decay attractive. The poet who is so often diacritical was attracted to the literary form that is so as well—attracted to the possibility of rechanneling the diacritical agenda of that form to pursue his more idiosyncratic preoccupation with rivalry. And the poet who was both resident and alien in so many areas of his life was drawn to the literary tradition that is at once inside and outside the norms of love poetry.

Notes

1. Arthur F. Marotti, in his *John Donne, Coterie Poet* (Madison: University of Wisconsin Press, 1986), 51–52, notes, however, that the evidence for assuming it was addressed to her is problematical. A lengthy discussion of that problem is outside my scope here.

2. For a summary of this background, see Helen Gardner's edition of the Elegies, at page 147.

3. Cathy Yandell, "Carpe Diem, Poetic Immortality, and the Gendered Ideology of Time," in *Renaissance Women Writers: French Texts/American Contexts*, ed. Anne R. Larson and Colette H. Winn (Detroit: Wayne State University Press, 1994).

4. See Donald L. Guss, "Donne's 'The Anagram': Sources and Analogues," *HLQ* 28 (1964): 79–82; and J. B. Leishman, *Monarch of Wit* (1951; rpt. London: Hutchinson, 1969), 77–84.

5. Compare Guibbory, " 'Oh, let mee not serve so,: The Politics of Love in Donne's *Elegies*," *ELH* 57 (1990): 817, on the ambivalence towards the speaker's lady.

6. On the debate about this issue, see Ian Maclean, *The Renaissance Notion of*

Woman: A Study in the Fortunes of Scholasticism and Medical Science in European Intellectual Life (Cambridge: Cambridge University Press, 1980), 35–37.

7. *OED*, s.v. "spermatic."

8. The argument about homology was established in Thomas Lacqueur's influential article "Orgasm, Generation, and the Politics of Reproductive Biology," *Representations*, no. 14 (1986): 1–41, and in his *Making Sex: Body and Gender form the Greeks to Freud* (Cambridge: Harvard University Press, 1990). For attacks on it, see Janet Adelman, "Suffocating Mothers: Galen, Hysteria, and the Discourse of the Maternal Body in—and out of—*King Lear*," paper delivered at the Shakespeare Association of America conference, Vancouver, Canada, March 1991; Katharine Park and Robert A. Nye, "Destiny Is Anatomy," review of *Making Sex* by Thomas Lacqueur, *New Republic*, February 18, 1991, 53–57; and my article "Navel Battles: Interpreting Renaissance Gynecological Manuals," *American Notes and Queries*, n.s. 5 (1992): 68–69.

9. See, e.g., Phyllis Rackin, "Androgyny, Mimesis, and the Marriage of the Boy Heroine on the English Renaissance Stage," *PMLA* 102 (1987): 29–41.

10. See Dubrow, *A Happier Eden: The Politics of Marriage in the Stuart Epithalamium* (Ithaca: Cornell University Press, 1990), 162–63.

11. On his neglect of mythology, cf. Hunt, *Donne's Poetry: Essays in Literary Analysis* (New Haven: Yale University Press 1954), 210 n.23; Leishman, *Monarch of Wit*, 19.

12. Compare Guibbory's observation that "The Anagram" and "The Comparison" draw attention to connections between the grotesque body and the beautiful one (" 'Oh, let mee not serve so,' " 815–17).

13. For a particularly thoughtful commentary on that debate, see Richard Strier, "John Donne Awry and Squint: The Holy Sonnets, 1608–1610," *MP* 86 (1989): 381–82.

To "build in sonnets pretty roomes"?: Donne and the Renaissance Love Lyric

N. H. KEEBLE

MANY DIFFERENT GENRES ARE SIGNALED BY THE TITLES OF DONNE'S POEMS, but lyric is not one of them. Indeed, the word was hardly available to him as a generic term. Although *lyre* is recorded in the *Oxford English Dictionary* from the thirteenth century, *lyric* as both adjective and substantive is known only from the 1580s, and even then the evidence for the noun is very slim. A passing reference to Surrey's *"Liricks"* in Sidney's *Apology for Poetry* is the only instance cited before the eighteenth century.[1] Where one might most expect to find it, in the many Renaissance categorizations of poetic genres, it is missing. When, for example, Dudley North associates poetic genres with musical forms, his comprehensive list of poetic kinds does not include the lyric: "Musick hath its Anthems, Pavens, Fantesies, Galliards, Courantoes, Ayres, Sarabands, Toyes, Cromatiques, etc. And Verses have their Hymns, Tragedies, Satyres, Heroiques, Sonets, Odes, Songs, Epigrams, Distiques, and Strong Lines, which are their Cromatiques."[2] The predominant usage was adjectival, as when William Webbe, following Horace and translating Georgius Fabricius, distinguishes as the "most vsuall kindes" of verse "the *Heroic*, the *Elegiac*, *Iambick*, and *Lyric*."[3] The noun is similarly missing when, in his chapter on the *"sundry formes"* of ancient poetry, George Puttenham writes of poets who "more delighted to write songs or ballads of pleasure, to be song with the voice, and to the harpe, lute, or citheron & such other musical instruments, they were called melodious Poets [*melici*] or by a more common name *Lirique* Poets." Puttenham knows of lyric poets, but they write songs and ballads, not lyrics.[4]

For Puttenham, then, the word *lyric* connoted not a genre but a mode.[5] It implied generic characteristics, suggesting a tendency towards the balladic and the songlike, but it denoted no specific form. Puttenham's examples of lyric poets—Pindar, Anacreon, Callimachus,

71

Horace, and Catullus—embrace a great variety of genres. Consequently, when Renaissance poets and rhetoricians wished to instance
specific cases of the lyrical, they used not its substantival form but a
variety of other generic terms. William Drummond of Hawthornden,
for example, published sonnets, songs, madrigals, and hymns, but no
lyrics. Michael Drayton explained in the dedication and preface to his
Odes with other Lyrick Poesies (1619) that he has so titled these "*Lyrick
Pieces*" because "an Ode is knowne to haue been properly a song,
moduled to the ancient harpe," "some transcendently loftie," such as
Pindar's, some "amorous, soft, and made for Chambers," such as Anacreon's, and some "of a mixed kinde," such as Horace's. His collection, he claims, follows Horace, but it admits also a "Skeltoniad," a
"canzonet," a "hymne," and, "dressed in the old English Garbe" of
Chaucer and of Spenser, a ballad—all "lyrick poesies."[6] Thomas Campion similarly refers to "*Ditties* or *Odes*; which we may call *Lyricall*,
because they are apt to be soong to an instrument, if they were
adorn'd with conuenient notes." He himself published not lyrics but
airs or, occasionally, songs. [7] Just so, remarking the dominance of dramatic poetry in contemporary England, Sidney observes that of
"Other sorts of Poetry almost haue we none, but that Lyricall kind of
Songs and Sonnets."[8]

Songs and Sonets was, of course, the heading under which Donne's
secular love poems came to be printed. This formulation, an inversion
of the heading "Sonnetts and Songes" in one of the manuscripts, first
appeared as a section heading in the second (1635) edition of the
poems, probably, as Helen Gardner conjectures, to recall "the most
famous sixteenth-century collection of love-poetry," *Songes and Sonet-
tes, written by the . . . late Earle of Surrey, and other* (1557), popularly
known after its publisher (and probable editor) as *Tottel's Miscellany*.
She takes the heading to signify "simply love lyrics.' "[9] If so, it is either
unwittingly inappropriate or knowingly ironic. With songs and sonnets, as they treat of love, the English Renaissance above all associated lyricism, courtliness, and what it was in the habit of terming
sweetness. For Puttenham, as we heard, lyric poets were the *melici*, the
honied ones. Wyatt and Surrey, the protagonists of *Tottel's Miscellany*,
he applauded for having introduced precisely this quality into English
verse, hailing them as "the first reformers of our English meeter" and
"the two chieftaines" of the "new company of courtly makers" that
"sprong up" in "the latter end" of Henry VII's reign who, "hauing trau-
ailed into Italie, and there tasted the sweete and stately measures and

stile of the Italian Poesie . . . greatly pollished our rude & homely manner of vulgar Poesie." Francis Meres famously spoke appreciatively of
Shakespeare's "sugred *Sonnets,*" and for Sidney the allure of poesy
was akin to the sweet enticement of "a cluster of Grapes." When, for
his own rhetorical ends, Sidney parodied the sonneteering habits of
sixteenth-century love poets, their "sweetest plaint" and "sweetest
stile" were among his targets.[10] Any reader encouraged by the heading
"Songs and Sonets" to anticipate the sacharrine in Donne's poems,
however, would have been sadly disappointed. Not only are there
very few songs in the "Songs and Sonets"—and, of course, no sonnets, strictly speaking—but Donne is never sweet or honied. Quite the
contrary: he can speak, as he does in "The triple Foole," of the "whin-
ing Poetry" of love, and of "Rimes vexation" (lines 3, 9), but never, like
George Herbert in "The Forerunners," of its "sweet phrases, lovely
metaphors," "Lovely enchanting language, sugar-cane, / Hony of
roses."[11] This restrained diet was much to his admirers' taste. In his
elegiac tribute, Thomas Carew applauded Donne's substitution of "a
line / Of masculine expression" for the "tun'd chime" and "soft melting Phrases" of the sugared style which so took with those contemporaries who, for Carew, are "superstitious fooles" enslaved to poetic
tradition.[12]

    Declining the lyrical mode advertised by their heading, the lyrics of
the "Songs and Sonets" are characterized instead by generic resis-
tance and subversion; their relationship to songs and sonnets is ironic
and parodic. With neither his texts, nor his readers, nor the women
whom he ostensibly addresses does Donne establish the relationship
expected of a sixteenth-century lyricist. He never presents himself as
a lutenist in the manner of Wyatt (or even Herbert in "Easter"), nor as
a harpist like Drayton, nor as a musician-lover, like Campion.[13] Ben
Jonson, like Donne a master of the asperic and curt, is yet willing to
present himself as a singer, to write lyrics set to music, to style his
poems *songs,* and to use the adjective *lyric* in his titles.[14] Not so
Donne,[15] who very rarely adopts a straightforwardly lyrical measure
and never shows any appreciation of songs or singing. The possibility
of his verse being set to music only increases his vexation in "The
triple Foole":

> Some man, his art and voice to show,
>   Doth Set and sing my paine,
> And, by delighting many, frees againe
>   Griefe, which verse did restraine.

> To Love, and Griefe tribute of Verse belongs,
> But not of such as pleases when 'tis read,
>   Both are increased by such songs:
>   For both their triumphs so are published
>
> (13–20)

Music, it seems, is very far from being the food of love. Donne here sits uncomfortably to lyrical verse and to the public performance of love songs.[16] The singer attracts the socially dismissive scorn ("some man") reserved, in "Loves Alchymie," for the sexual activities of "my man" servant (line 15). We may conjecture Donne's opinion of Alphonso Ferrabosco's *Ayres* (1609), in which "The Expiration" did appear with musical accompaniment, very different to that of Jonson's deeply appreciative prefatory poem.[17] The indecorous colloquiality of Donne's poems, the cacophonies and the extravagantly modulated meters which Carew so appreciated but so offended Jonson ("Donne, for not keeping of accent, deserved hanging")[18] may be taken as a determined rebuttal of the lyrical and the songlike.[19] Certainly Donne's own characterizations of himself as a writer of verses "too'harsh for rime" ("To Mr. T.W.: All haile sweet Poet," 25) repudiate any suggestion of the mellifluous: "I sing not, Siren like, to tempt; for I / Am harsh" ("To Mr. S. B.," 9–10). Despite that heading "Songs and Sonets," Donne stubbornly resists the company of Puttenham's "melodious" lyric poets.

He is to be found rather among Puttenham's love poets. Love poetry, writes Puttenham,

> requireth a forme of Poesie variable, inconstant, affected, curious and most witty of any others, whereof the ioyes were to be vttered in one sorte, the sorrowes in an other, and by the many formes of Poesie, the many moodes and pangs of louers, throughly to be discouered: the poore soules sometimes praying, beseeching, sometime honouring, auancing, praising: an other while railing, reviling, and cursing: then sorrowing, weeping, lamenting: in the ende laughing, reioysing & solacing the beloued againe, with a thousand delicate deuises, odes, songs, elegies, ballads, sonets, and other ditties, mouing one way and another to great compassion.[20]

Here, while the lyrical is reserved for one particular kind of love poem, the celebration of the joy of love, the body of love poetry is characterized by its unpredictability and its variety. Drayton agreed: in the introductory sonnet to his sequence *Idea*, he avers that "My Verse is the true image of my Mind, / Euer in motion, still desiring change; / And as thus to Varietie inclin'd / So in all Humors sportively I range."[21] This, though, is an apter account of Donne's program than of Drayton's, who visits far fewer humors, and less sportingly. And Donne far better illustrates the third quality Puttenham identifies: wit. In this respect, the appeal of the heading "Songs and Sonets" to *Tottel's Miscellany* was as poor a marketing ploy as it was a guide to the nature of Donne's poems. By the 1630s *Tottel's Miscellany* was very old hat. Its title page had been baldly descriptive, relying on the appeal of Surrey's name to promote sales. Anthologies of love poetry had long since sought readers by quite a different strategy. Such title pages as *The Paradyce of Daynty Devyses* (1576), *A Gorgeous Gallery of Gallant Inventions* (1578), *The Phoenix Nest* (1593), *England's Helicon* (1600), and *A Poeticall Rhapsody* (1602) promise inspiration, inventiveness, and wit. The same was true of single-authored collections: when Campion published a collection of divine and secular songs in *Two Bookes of Ayres* ([1612?]) he distinguished them respectively as "morall songs' and "light conceits of lovers," where *conceit* again promises ingenuity, pointedness, even as *light* properly deprives the enterprise of seriousness.[22]

Generically, wit was characteristic not of songs but of the tersely elliptical and dramatically abrupt epigram:

> in which euery mery conceited man might, without any long studie or tedious ambage, make his frend sport, and anger his foe, and giue a prettie nip, or shew a sharpe conceit in few verses: for this *Epigramme* is but an inscription or writting made as it were vpon a table, or in a windowe, or vpon the wall or mantell or a chimney in some place of common resort, where it was allowed euery man might come, or be sitting to chat and prate, as now in our tauernes and common tabling houses, where many merry heades meete, and scrible with ynke, with chalke, or with a cole, such matters as they would euery man should know & descant vpon.[23]

The context created here, a combination of the Boar's Head with the Mermaid, hits off Donne exactly: witty, satiric and parodic, performative, masculine, casual and colloquial, urban and middle-class.[24] What it misses is the intense privacy of Donne: when, in "A Valediction: of my Name in the Window," Donne indeed scratches something on a pane of glass, it is not, as in Puttenham, in "a place of common resort" for "euery man" to see but in a private house and for one person's eyes.[25]

While there was a general feeling that curtness and a certain colloquial gracelessness distinguished the plain style of the epigram from
the lyricism of the sonnet,[26] the absence of the sonnet from the classical repertoire of genres upon which Renaissance thinking depended
facilitated its assimilation into, elision with, or contamination by the
epigram, causing considerable headaches to Renaissance critics trying
to distinguish the two. The epigrammatic possibilities of the final couplet of the English sonnet and the free use of the terms *epigram* and
sonnet of poems between four and sixteen lines in length regardless of
rhyme scheme contributed to the confusion and to the creation of a
hybrid genre.[27] Rosalie Colie observes that Joseph Scaliger categorized epigrams as *fel* (gall), *acetum* (vinegar), *sal* (salt), and *mel* (honey),
and that the sonnet's incorporation of these qualities extended its
range and counterpointed its sweetness. She mentions Shakespeare
but much the more radical case is Donne.[28] Twenty of his own epigrams are extant, and sudden unexpected turns of thought, paradox,
and "the solidity of epigrammatic closure"[29] mark Donne's love
poems far more than they do Shakespeare's.[30] Drummond of Hawthornden recognized that "if he would, [Donne] might easily be the best
Epigrammatist we have found in *English*," while Jonson publicly acknowledged Donne the "best authority" to judge Jonson's own epigrams and the person whose approval would confer lasting poetic
fame.[31] They had taken Donne's measure more accurately than the
person responsible for the heading "Songs and Sonets," which reinstates the very generic allegiance that Donne's own authorial choices
had refused.

That refusal is enacted both by the shape of the collection at large
and by the form of individual poems. Something more than Renaissance *sprezzatura* lay behind Donne's dismissive remark in a letter to
Henry Goodyer that "The Spanish proverb informs me, that he is a
fool which cannot make one Sonnet, and he is mad which makes two,"
for he was at pains to avoid any association with the galaxy of Elizabethan sonneteers.[32] Though writing in the 1590s, in the heyday of the
sonnet-sequence vogue which attracted Spenser, Sidney, Shakespeare, Drayton, Daniel, and a host of their lesser contemporaries,
Donne pointedly ignored current fashion, eschewing both the sonnet
sequence and the sonnet in his secular love poetry. For the effusions
of the *melici*, with what he saw as their tired Petrarchan conventionali-
ties, Donne had only disdain:[33] it may well have been a sonnet sequence of this sort that prompted the contemptuous derision of poetry

in Satire II.[34] This independence is declared still more forcefully by the forms Donne chose to adopt in place of the formal predictability of the sonnet sequence and the regular iambic quatrains of the lyric. The structural inventiveness and diversity of his love poems is commonly remarked, but not their radical implication in an age when literary aesthetics, criticism, and reading were all generically structured. For the received lyrical genres Donne substituted a metrical and stanzaic variety unprecedented in any collection of English love poetry. Formally, his short love poems are at the farthest possible remove from "Songs and Sonets." Each successive poem finds yet another way to declare itself not a sonnet. In this respect, they delivered a resounding generic rebuff to the lyrical and sonneteering tradition of the Renaissance, and one that proved fatal.[35]

Though striking, such formal idiosyncracy and unpredictability is of a piece with other kinds of indecorum. Whereas Spenser began with pastoral and moved, in proper Virgilian fashion, to epic, and even Shakespeare from sonnets and comedy to tragedy, Donne remains with the lightest and least of genres, as Renaissance critics categorized the various kinds of short poem. Defending poetry in the preface to his translation of *Orlando Furioso*, Harrington conceded that, unlike epic and tragedy, "the Pastorall with the Sonnet or Epigramme" is guilty of "lightnes & wantonnes." Though "delightful," "many times they sauour of wantonnes and loue and toying, and, now and then breaking the rules of Poetry, go into plaine scurrilitie."[36] This is Donne's generic territory: he has absolutely no epic pretensions. He no more aspires to what Sidney called "the best and most accomplished kind of poetry" than he assumes the morally didactic role Sidney, in typical Renaissance fashion, ascribed to the poet: "I will have no such Readers as I can teach," Donne impatiently declared.[37] To flout in this way the formal and didactic seriousness of poetry signals a wider subversiveness. The generic hierarchy and the notion of generic decorum were closely allied to social order and decorum: to infringe one was to affront the other.[38] And Donne does affront. His poetic persona lacks respect. To center his poetic concerns Donne will marginalize all that his contemporaries prized—the discovery of America, shall we say ("Let sea-discoverers to new worlds have gone. . . ."), the professions ("Lawyers finde out still / Litigious men . . ."), intellectual and religious ideas—the famed metaphysical conceit is founded on a disrespectful readiness to misapply concepts, no matter how sacred the doctrine ("love . . . transubstantiates all") or blasphemous the effect ("and I / A something else").[39] For insisting on decorum and order, the supreme celestial body, the sun—emblem of regality, divinity, and hierarchy—is scorned in "The Sunne Rising" as an "unruly," "Sawcy pedantique wretch," a "Busie old foole," an impotent irrelevance: "Must to thy motions lovers seasons run . . ." (1–5).

In that poem, kings, courts, and their entertainments are put on a par with the activities of "countrey ants" (5–8). This is characteristic: Donne is most especially impatient with social superiors, with the court and all its doings. In his second and fourth satires, those "Which dwell at Court" epitomize the vicious, corrupt, and deceitful ("Satyre IV," 16). In the verse letters, too, "vertue" in "Courtiers hearts / Suffers an Ostracisme, and departs" ("To the Countesse of Bedford: T'have written then," 21–22). This is unexceptional in Elizabethan satire, but the continuance of such contempt in the "Songs and Sonets" lends them a radical social and political charge foreign to the Elizabethan lyric. Here, too, "truth" is foreign to courts ("The Will," 11). The court and courtliness are central to *Astophil and Stella;* in "Songs and Sonets" they are marginalized. The business of the town counts for more than their elaborate entertainments and manners; present emotion presses more strongly than the rituals of patronage. It is from the court and its preoccupations that in "The Canonization" Donne withdraws: to 'Take . . . a course, get . . . a place, / Observe his honour or his grace, / And the Kings reall, or his stamped face / Contemplate" is a far lesser thing than Donne and his lover enjoy (5–8). "All Kings, and all their favourites" are deprived of their status when "Here upon earth, we'are Kings, and none but wee / Can be such Kings' ("The Anniversarie," 1, 23–27). The disdain that had fueled satiric contempt now reinforces the valorization of the lovers' experience as, in a Platonic parody, received ideological values are inverted: "Princes doe but play us" ("The Sunne Rising," 23). Donne's linguistic register is as different to Sidney's as is his social milieu. The harshness of that "masculine style" is itself insolent. Its gracelessness is a social affront; it is no way to talk in polite society.[40] If Herbert's lyrics are the politest in the language, Donne's are the rudest.

As is often remarked, Donne is similarly disrespectful towards what as a rule most overawed the male Renaissance love poet: his mistress. He can speak appreciatively, but of the experience of love with her, never of her. The blazon, upon which so much rhetorical ingenuity was spent, is no part of his poetic repertoire. He never attempts anything like sonnets 64 of the *Amoretti* or 9 of *Astrophil and Stella*, or the earlier of Shakespeare's sonnets, on the loved one's beauty.[41] "Image of her whom I love" have we none ("Elegie X. The Dreame," 1). Indeed, she is never even named, never accorded one of those Greco-Latinate romance names Elizabethan and Cavalier poets favored, and Donne (no more than any other English Renaissance poet) dare not match the biographical openness of Spenser's Elizabeth. And so, we can never tell what relationship contextualizes the encounters in the poems.[42] If, however, there is no better example of absent female presence than Donne's love poetry, the insistently present masculine voice is hardly that of the male Renaissance lover. Donne is not inclined to adopt the male lover's imploring and deferential posture—the only posture known, for example, to Samuel Daniel, who, in the fifty sonnets of his *Delia* (1592), takes his "vnhappy pen" to write "a volume of despayres, / The wayling Iliades of my tragicke wo" which tell of the "liuing death" of loving a "stony harte" and of the "Tears, vowes, and prayers" with which he passes "the Aprill of my yeers in wayling" and in vain address to the "cruell She."[43] Such limp lamentations Donne's hectoring no-nonsense manliness and insistent libido impatiently reject in a verse letter to the countess of Huntingdon:

> neither will I vexe your eyes to see
> A sighing Ode, nor cross-arm'd Elegie.
> I come not to call pitty from your heart,
> Like some white-liver'd dotard that would part
> Else from his slipperie soule with a faint groane,
> And faithfully, (without you smil'd) were gone.
> I cannot feele the tempest of a frowne,
> I may be rais'd by love, but not throwne down.
> Though I can pittie those sigh twice a day,
> I hate that thing whispers it selfe away.
> ("To the Countesse of Huntingdon: That unripe side," 21–30)

In "Songs and Sonets," the fraught and pained suit of a Daniel is reduced to an inconsequential performance: "I spring a mistresse, sweare, write, sigh and weepe: / And the game kill'd, or lost, goe talke, and sleepe" ("Loves diet," 29–30).

And, as he cannot tolerate the lover's pose, so Donne avoids the commonest location of the Renaissance lover's laments and the lyric's habitual pastoralism. We are rarely outside in Donne, and never in fields, arbors or groves, strolling by streams, singing madrigals, or minding sheep. When we do venture outdoors, it is to have our ge-

neric expectations frustrated. In Donne, gardens quite fail to solace
rejected lovers ("Twicknam Garden"), flowers do not prompt analo-
gies for female beauty ("The Blossome") nor do walks allow the contemplation of natural scenes ("A Lecture upon the Shadow"). There is
a "Pregnant banke" in "The Exstasie" but it occupies only a line or
two (2) and its intimation of the asexual (or supra-sexual) emotional
and spiritual succour common in pastoral is subverted by the poem's
subsequent vindication of the body. Like its neoplatonism, the poem's
pastoralism is part of a beguiling strategy by which it seeks to introduce the material, the physical, and the sexual. Donne is as impatient
of gardens as he is of courts (and neoplatonism): he would far rather
get back to urban scenes, and to a bit of action. Only the plague, when
"pleasures dirth our City doth posses," can drive him from town into
the country, "Pleasure, now fled from London, to retrive' ("To Mr.
E.G.," 7, 14). Nor will he stay any longer than he has to. His exasper-
ated exclamation in "The Blossome" carries us from gardens, and
from women, back to Puttenham's epigrammatic tavern scene: "Meet
mee at London, then, / Twenty dayes hence, and thou shalt see / Mee
fresher, and more fat, by being with men, / Then if I had staid still
with her and thee" (34–7).[44] And in the city, as soon as he is there, he
would get himself indoors. A bedroom supplies the analogy for that
bank in "The Exstasie" ("Where, like a pillow on a bed"), and that
rather than a garden is the locus of Donne's love poetry. It is preferred
not merely to pastoral fields but to the entirety of outdoor experience:
when "All" is "here in one bed," "Nothing else is." This conceit culminates in the Donnean cosmology of "The Sunne Rising," which resolves the contention between rival heliocentric and geocentric
cosmologies not with the angelic reticence of Milton's Raphael but
with the jouissance of a bed-centred—that is, self-centred—system
("This bed thy center is, these walls, thy spheare," (20, 22, 30).

It is the intensity of the private experience of love that centers beds
rather than courts (or gardens) in this poetry; that is what "makes one
little roome, an every where" ("The good-morrow," 11). When, in
"The Canonization," the public world of the court is rejected, it is
not—as by the satires of Wyatt, Spenser, or Ralegh, or by Donne's
own satires—in hope of a commonwealth finer than the Tudor but for
the private world of love. Compared to that "Nothing else is": privacy
is given an all-annihilating centrality. Donne's recurrent clerical and
monastic imagery of renunciation and of sanctification is directed
towards an unworldly elevation and eremitical isolation of the lov-

ers—"one anothers hermitage"—in death and the grave, if need be.[45] Seclusion and privacy are hence keynotes in ways quite foreign to the generality of sixteenth-century songs and sonnets.[46] It is the *publishing* of his love that Donne detests in "The triple Foole," and his refusal to name the woman betokens a kind of secrecy, a determination to withhold even as the poem declares: "Who ever guesses, thinks, or dreames he knowes / Who is my mistris, wither by this curse" ("The Curse," 1–2). For all his declamatory posturing and intellectual histrionics, the Donne of "Songs and Sonets" is curiously reticent about his lover and their relationship, withholding them from the reader's gaze, "I" and "we" from "them."[47] The poems never imply a large public readership. Their immediate addressee, within their rhetorical fictions, is always a single person—a woman usually, but occasionally a friend or an apostrophized object or the poet's self—never, directly, the reader.

In these respects, the "Songs and Sonets" have another boundary, contiguous not with the epigram but with epistles, elegies, and satires—the very genres with which, of course, Donne began his career: all of them in their various degrees conversationally informal, irreverent, intimate, and all of them touching ideas and essaying positions, particularly Ovidian and anti-courtly, which recur in the "Songs and Sonets."[48] The couplets of these longer poems allow a more sustained development of ideas than is possible in the epigram and a greater complexity of attitude than is possible in lyric. It is this combination of the epigrammatic with the elegiac which Alastair Fowler sees as creating the "witty pointed love elegy that we know as Metaphysical lyric." This description, as David Lindley remarks, may sound "somewhat Polonian,"[49] still more so if we add, as we should, satire ("The Will," for example, has the very note of Ralegh), but there is one constant in this generic elusiveness: it conjures the spoken voice. It is a genre centred not on the singing but on the speaking voice,[50] and commonly the speaking voice in argumentative mode. Donne does not sing, he argues, relentlessly and on any topic, but from such premises and with such logical leaps and fantastical surmises that the seriousness of his contentions is always open to question. They demand not merely aural response at one sitting but to be tussled with over and over. They are to be privately read, not publicly performed.[51] The challenge and frustration of their obscurity was recognized by their first readers, not always appreciatively; Donne, "for not being understood, would perish," said Jonson. It was precisely the generic indecorum of his "affecting the metaphysics" in "amorous verses" which affronted so decorous a poet as Dryden.[52]

As these rather irritated comments illustrate, Donne's speaking voice can be contrary and perverse: his poems are neither single-minded nor unproblematically univocal: although "I" speak all the time, "I" am Protean. Donne is no more forthcoming about himself than about his lover. He never identifies himself with his poetic voice like Jonson, and never (like Sidney and Spenser), encourages an asso-ciation of the poetic "I" with the biographical self. Jonson can write of his son and daughter, but not Donne; Jonson "of all styles . . . loved most to be named honest," but Donne *did best when I had least truth for my subjects.*"[53] Where Sidney teases with references to Sidney arms and puns on the name Rich, Donne's persona mentions not one spe-cific biographical detail. Where the first person of the *Amoretti* has written a poem called *The Faerie Queene*, the poetic "I" of the "Songs and Sonets" only vaguely gestures towards "all that I in Ryme have writ' ("The Will," 32).[54] Cut free from autobiography, the "Songs and Sonets" are fictions in which Donne tries on a succession of masks, acts a series of roles; this is crucial to the pronominal complexity of a poem like "The Legacie."[55] That is why Donne is so mercurial, chame-leon-like, untroubled by contradiction. For all the persuasiveness of their speaking voice, the "Songs and Sonets" anticipate not the subjec-tivity which was to become the lyrical standard of the romantics[56] but the monologues of Browning, which Browning himself designated dra-matic rather than lyrical.[57] They are, like Browning's poems, "so many utterances of so many imaginary persons," and so, of course, in the line to Eliot—who, with a generic inappropriateness to equal the ti-tling of Donne's love poems "Songs and Sonets," accorded J. Alfred Prufrock a love *song*.

NOTES

1. *OED*, s.v. *Lyre¹*; *Lyric, a.* and *sb.*; *Lyrical, a.*; Sir Philip Sidney, *An Apologie for Poetrie* (1595), in *Elizabethan Critical Essays*, ed. G. Gregory Smith, 2 vols. (Oxford: Clarendon Press, 1904), 1:196 (and in *Miscellaneous Prose of Sir Philip Sidney*, ed. Kath-erine Duncan-Jones and Jan Van Dorsten [Oxford: Clarendon Press, 1973], 112). Other forms (*lyricist*, etc.) are eighteenth- or nineteenth-century coinages.

2. [Dudley North], *A Forest of Varieties* (1645), 3, quoted in Rosalie L. Colie, *The Resources of Kind: Genre-Theory in the Renaissance*, ed. Barbara K. Lewalski (Berkeley and Los Angeles: University of California Press, 1973), 6.

3. William Webbe, *A Discourse of English Poetrie* (1586), in Smith, ed., *Elizabethan*

Critical Essays, 1:291 (Fabricius' original is printed on 1:417). So, too, Sidney: "The most notable bee the *Heroick, Lirick, Tragick, Comick, Satirick, Iambick, Elegiack, Pastorall*, and certaine others" (*Apologie*, in Smith, ed., *Elizabethan Critical Essays*, 1:159 [and in *Miscellaneous Prose of Sir Philip Sidney*, 81]), followed by Francis Meres, *Palladis Tamia, Wits Treasury* (1598) (in Smith, ed., *Elizabethan Critical Essays*, 2:319). Such Renaissance systems of generic classification variously conflate Aristotle, Quintillian, Cicero, Horace, and Diomedes: see Alastair Fowler, *Kinds of Literature: An Introduction to the Theory of Genre and Modes* (Oxford: Clarendon Press, 1982), 216–21 and n. 22; E. R. Curtius, *European Literature and the Latin Middle Ages*, trans. Willard R. Trask (London: Routledge, 1953), 440–43.

4. [George Puttenham], *The Arte of English Poesie (1589)* (Menston: Scolar, 1968), 20 (and in Smith, ed., *Elizabethan Critical Essays*, 2:26).

5. This is to adopt the distinction made by Fowler, *Kinds of Literature*, 55–56, 106–9, 137.

6. William Drummond of Hawthornden, *The Works* (Edinburgh: James Watson, 1711), 2nd pagination, 1–35; [Puttenham], *Arte of English Poesie*, 20 (and in Smith, ed., *Elizabethan Critical Essays*, 2: 26); Michael Drayton, *Poems [1619]* (Menston: Scolar, 1969), 277, 279–80, 301, 303, 305.

7. Thomas Campion, *Obseruations in the Art of English Poesie* (1602), in Percival Vivian, ed., *Campion's Works* (Oxford: Clarendon Press, 1909), vi–vii, 49 (and in Smith, ed., *Elizabethan Critical Essays*, 2:346). In its musical sense, denoting light and usually solo songs, *air*, like *lyric*, was a neologism in the 1590s (*OED, s.v. Air*, 19).

8. Sidney, *Apologie*, in Smith, ed., *Elizabethan Critical Essays*, 1:201 (and in *Miscellaneous Prose of Sir Philip Sidney*, 116).

9. John Donne, *The Elegies and Songs and Sonnets*, ed. Helen Gardner (Oxford: Clarendon Press, 1965), xlvii, 151.

10. [Puttenham], *Arte of English Poesie*, 48–49; Meres, in Smith, ed., *Elizabethan Critical Essays*, 2:317; Sidney, *Apologie*, in Smith, ed., *Elizabethan Critical Essays*, 1:172 (and in *Miscellaneous Prose of Sir Philip Sidney*, 92); Sidney, *Astrophil and Stella*, sonnet 6, in *The Poems of Sir Philip Sidney*, ed. William A. Ringler (Oxford: Clarendon Press, 1962), 168.

11. George Herbert, *The Works*, ed. F. E. Hutchinson (1941; Oxford: Clarendon Press, 1964), 41–42, 176. For Herbert, *sweetness* remained a positive quality, and *sweet* a favourite adjective, connoting innocence and grace in persons, beauty in nature and articulacy in poetry; see the listings in Mario di Cesare and Rigo Magnani, ed., *A Concordance to the Complete Writings of George Hebert* (Ithaca and London: Cornell University Press, 1977).

12. "An Elegie upon the death of . . . Dr. John Donne," lines 38–39, 41, 46, 53, in *The Satires, Epigrams and Verse Letters of John Donne*, ed. W. Milgate (Oxford: Clarendon Press, 1967), 89.

13. On the lyric and song, and the continuing fiction of the lyrical singer, see W. R. Johnson, *The Idea of the Lyric: Lyric Modes in Ancient and Modern Poetry* (Berkeley and Los Angeles: University of California Press, 1982).

14. E.g., "A Celebration of Charis in Ten Lyric Pieces" (*The Poems*, ed. George Parfitt [Harmondsworth: Penguin, 1975], 126–35) and such lyrics as *Poems*, 103–4, 106–7, 135–39, 171–72, 227–29.

15. The only instance of the word *lyric* in his poetry given in Homer Carrol Combs and Zay Ruck Sullens, ed., *A Concordance to the English Poetry of John Donne* (Chicago: Packard, 1940) is the unremarkable "lirique Larke" in "An Epithalamion . . . on the Lady Elizabeth . . . ," line 6.

16. On the interrelations of the singing of lyrics, music, and courtly love, see John Stevens, *Music & Poetry in the Early Tudor Court* (Cambridge: Cambridge University Press, 1979).

17. Jonson, epigram 130, in *Poems,* 85 (and cf. epigram 131). Gardner, *Elegies and Songs and Sonnets,* appendix B, 238–41, identifies six of Donne's songs and sonnets said to have been written to existing tunes: "Song: 'Goe, and catch a falling starre,' " "The Message," "Song: 'Sweetest love, I do not goe,' " "The Baite," "Communitie," "Confined Love," for which the settings for the first four are extant. "The Expiration" is, with "Break of Day" and "The Apparition," one of three poems known to have been set to music in the seventeenth century (241–44). Cf. Theodore Redpath, ed., *The Songs and Sonets of John Donne,* 2nd ed. (London: Methuen, 1983), appendix 12, 341–43.

18. *Ben Jonson's Conversations with William Drummond of Hawthornden,* in *Poems,* 462.

19. This point is made in Arnold Stein, *John Donne's Lyrics* (Minneapolis: University of Minnesota Press, 1962), 20.

20. [Puttenham], *Arte of English Poesie,* 36.

21. Drayton, *Poems,* 252.

22. Campion, *Observations,* vi, 111.

23. [Puttenham], *Arte of English Poesie,* 43 (and in Smith, ed., *Elizabethan Critical Essays,* 2:56). The passage is from Puttenham's 26th chapter, on *"The manner of Poesie by which they uttered their bitter taunts, and priuy nips, or witty scoffes and other merry conceits."*

24. In his *Epigrams* (1616), however, Jonson has in mind a more restrained and morally serious model. Epigram II, "To My Book," seeks to disabuse readers of precisely Puttenham's characterization of the genre. Jonson there directs his text to "Deceive [the] malice" of readers who from its title expect his collection "should'st be bold, licentious, full of gall, / Wormwood, and sulpher, sharp, and toothed withal" (*Poems,* 35; cf. epigram 18, p. 40).

25. This is discussed further on p. 80–81.

26. See, e.g., Fowler, *Kinds of Literature,* 138.

27. Fowler, *Kinds of Literature,* 183–84. E.g., George Gascoigne, *Certayne Notes of Instruction* (1575), in Smith, ed., *Elizabethan Critical Essays,* 1:55: "some thinke that all Poemes (being short) may be called Sonets, as in deede it is a diminutiue worde deriued of *Sonare.*"

28. Colie, *Resources of Kind,* 68, 69–75, 103; cf. Fowler, *Kinds of Literature,* 137–39.

29. David Lindley, *The Lyric* (London: Methuen, 1985), 10 (said of Donne).

30. Cf. Fowler, *Kinds of Literature,* 198–99: "Metaphysical style is from one point of view simply the style of epigram . . . when Metaphysical poetry is treated in terms of 'lyric' it often proves difficult or even disgusting."

31. Drummond of Hawthornden, *Works,* 226, cited in *Elegies and Songs and Sonnets,* Gardner, ed., xxvi n. 2, observing that "the development of Donne's art might be described in one way as his learning how to expand and enrich epigrammatic themes without losing the point and pungency that is characteristic of epigram"; Jonson, epigram 96, in *Poems,* 67–68.

32. R. C. Bald, *John Donne: A Life* (Oxford: Clarendon Press, 1970), 179–80.

33. John Carey, *John Donne: Life, Mind and Art* (London: Faber, 1981), 10, instances "To the Countess of Salisbury, August 1614," lines 3–7, to this effect.

34. The anonymous *Zepheria* (1594); see the editorial note in Milgate, ed., *Satires, Epigrams and Verse Letters,* 129–30.

35. The love sonnet barely survived the sixteenth century; it is not a metaphysical genre, and Milton's sonnets are predominantly public poems of a very different sort. Fowler, *Kinds of Literature*, 217, notes that by the early eighteenth century *sonneteer* had become a denigratory term for an inconsiderable poet.

36. Sir John Harrington, *A Preface, or rather a Briefe Apologie of Poetrie* (1591), in Smith, ed., *Elizabethan Critical Essays*, 2:209, quoted in Fowler, *Kinds of Literature*, 216–17.

37. Sidney, *Apologie*, in Smith, ed., *Elizabethan Critical Essays*, 1:179 (and in *Miscellaneous Prose of Sir Philip Sidney*, 98); Donne, prefatory epistle to "Metempsycosis," in *Poems*, 403.

38. Fowler, *Kinds of Literature*, 35.

39. *Seriatim* "The good-morrow," 12; "The Canonisation," 16–17; "Twicknam Garden," 6; "The Relique," 17–18.

40. Stein, *John Donne's Lyrics*, 24–25; cf. Douglas L. Peterson, *The English Lyric from Wyatt to Donne* (Princeton: Princeton University Press, 1967), 286–88 (citing Stein).

41. A point often made, as by Carey, *John Donne*, 9–10: "The physical characteristics of the girl he's supposed to be talking to don't concern him at all. Nor does her personality: it is completely obliterated in Donne's."

42. "Twicknam Garden" is a partial exception, in that the title refers to the countess of Bedford's property, but there is no mention of this fact, or of her, in the text itself and, in any case, the title does not appear in all manuscripts (others have "In a Garden") and there is no reason to suppose it Donne's (Gardner, ed., *Elegies and Songs and Sonnets*, 215, 248–51). Cf. Carey, *John Donne*, 79–80, 81: the poem relates to the real countess of Bedford "not at all."

43. Samuel Daniel, *Delia* (Menston: Scolar, 1969), *seriatim* sonnets 49, 39, 9, 13, 27, 11.

44. Cf. the remark that Donne was "clubbable," enjoying male company, in Carey, *John Donne*, 75. It is often remarked that Donne is a London poet (e.g., Peterson, *English Lyric*, 287), notably by Barbara Everett, in a 1972 lecture reprinted in her *Poets in their Time* (London: Faber, 1986), 1–31.

45. The point is often made: see, e.g., *Elegies and Songs and Sonnets*, Gardner, ed., lx.

46. Earl Miner, *The Metaphysical Mode from Donne to Cowley* (Princeton: Princeton University Press, 1969), 3–47, identifies and discusses "the private mode" as "the most distinctive, and distinguishing, feature of Metaphysical poetry," marking it off both from Elizabethan and from cavalier poetry (3). This idea is endorsed and developed by Anthony Low, *The Reinvention of Love: Poetry, Politics and Culture from Sidney to Milton* (Cambridge: Cambridge University Press, 1993), 48–59.

47. Cf. Miner, *Metaphysical Mode*, 5, and Carey, *John Donne*, 98–99, on the pronouns in Donne's love poetry.

48. As is often remarked; see, e.g., Miner, *Metaphysical Mode*, 7–11, 159–213 *passim; Elegies and Songs and Sonnets*, Gardner, ed., introduction, *passim*.

49. Fowler, *Kinds of Literature*, 222; Lindley, *The Lyric*, 11.

50. This has become "almost a cliché of Donne criticism," as John Hollander remarks in a chapter on "Donne and the Limits of Lyric" in *Vision and Resonance: Two Senses of Poetic Form* (New York: Oxford University Press, 1975), 44–58.

51. Rosemond Tuve, *Elizabethan and Metaphysical Imagery* (Chicago: University of Chicago Press, 1947), 242, associates Donne with "the slow establishment of a reading rather than a listening public during the hundred years of printing."

52. *Jonson's Conversations with Drummond of Hawthornden*, in *Poems* 466; John Dryden, *A Discourse concerning . . . Satire* (1693), in *John Dryden: Selected Criticism*, ed. James Kinsley and George Parfitt (Oxford: Clarendon Press, 1970), 211. The most searching discussion of Donne's thoughtfulness and argumentativeness, their contrariness and complexity, remains Carey, *John Donne*, where see especially 231–60.

53. Jonson, *Poems*, 478; Donne, letter to Sir Robert Carr accompanying "An Hymne to the Saints, and to Marquesse Hamylton," in *Poems*, 395.

54. Cf. Lindley, *The Lyric*, 59–61, in the course of his discussion of "The Lyric 'I.' "

55. Discussed by Carey, *John Donne*, 188–89, in the course of reflections upon Donne's sense of the "fluidity" of human individuality.

56. It was because he failed to meet the romantic criteria of the mellifluously evocative and subjectively authentic that Donne was excluded from the most influential anthology of lyrical poetry ever published in English, Francis Palgrave's *The Golden Treasury of the Best Songs and Lyrical Poems in the English Language* (1861).

57. Robert Browning, note to "Cavalier Tunes," *Bells and Pomegranates III: Dramatic Lyrics* (1842) in *The Complete Works*, ed. Roma A. King, 13 vols. in progress (Athens: Ohio University Press, 1969–   ) 3:197. Donne has been associated with Browning before—e.g., by Hollander, *Vision and Resonance*, 44–46.

The Holy Sonnets

F. W. Brownlow

Whatever second thoughts the english began to have a few years later, they greeted James VI and I's accession enthusiastically. With him and his family, royal domesticity—something not seen in England since Henry VIII's divorce—returned to the palace, and there was no more anxiety over the succesion. The long war with Spain ended, and the Hampton Court Conference of 1604 seemed to signal a change in religious life as well. Elizabeth I had never cared much for clerical company, preferring soldiers and athletes. James on the other hand liked being head of the Church of England, and he enjoyed talking to chaplains and bishops. One predictable result of his interest in the church, its personnel and management, was that for the first time the state church became fashionable, and Anglican devotion acquired chic.

As a dependent of Chancellor Egerton, John Donne would have been well placed to benefit from the change of regime when it came. The son of a famously Catholic family, with good reason to fear the menacing atmosphere of the court in Elizabeth's last decade, he was just the sort of person who would have found a more accepting environment under James. Unfortunately, even James's court could not accept a man who had clandestinely married his employer's niece while she was a minor child living under his protection. This irrevocable breach of the code of honor cut Donne off from any possibility of court office—as the king himself pointed out to Lord Hay in 1608.[1]

Walton explained Donne's marriage and his consequent failure to find secular employment as evidence of providential design: Donne's errors, like St. Augustine's, were the necessary prelude to his religious life, so that when he accepted ordination in 1615, "The *English Church* had gain'd a second St. *Austine,* for I think none was so like him before his conversion."[2]

Another explanation of Donne's ordination is that by 1615 he had no other option if he was to support his family. Entangled as the religious and secular spheres were in seventeenth-century England, in some respects they were quite distinct. For instance, the code of honor did not govern ecclesiastical appointments. In fact, Donne probably resisted ordination as long as he did because the church was no career for a man of honor—and as Dennis Flynn has proved, the young Donne saw himself, and was seen by others, as one who lived by the honor code.[3] In Donne's world, one could debate religion, and write poems and controversial treatises upon it without wishing to be an ecclesiastic. Readers who know the upshot of Donne's life naturally read his religious writing from the decade before his ordination as part of the mental process that led to it, but there is no evidence that Donne saw it that way.[4] He still had hopes of court employment as late as 1610, when he published *Pseudomartyr,* a book written to demonstrate mastery of civil and canon law as well as loyalty and a sound religious attitude.

The religious poems that Donne began to write circa 1608 reflect his involvement with a circle of courtly friends. His verse letters to Lady Bedford imply that he turned to religious poetry in response to changing court tastes. In the early days of their friendship, she acquired a copy of his satires from Ben Jonson, and the verse letter referring to her interest in these poems congratulates her on "[hallowing] a Pagan Muse," and flatters her as the embodiment of the court's new virtue:

> So whether my hymnes you admit or chuse,
> In me you'have hallowed a Pagan Muse,
> And denizend a stranger, who mistaught
> By blamers of the times they mard, hath sought
> Vertues in corners, which now bravely doe
> Shine in the worlds best part, or all It; You.
>
> (*Poems,* 273)

That is a compliment to the new court as well as the countess; Donne probably hoped she would pass it on. The poem presents Donne as an enthusiastic convert to the mystique of court culture, according to which intellectual and cultural life would thrive in the benign atmosphere of Stuart patronage. As a fashionable and pious ornament of James's court, the countess wanted hymns, epistles, and love poems from Donne, not satires. Ordination lay well in the unknown future when Donne was writing religious poetry as a clever layman for Lady Bedford and other people who counted on him to produce witty, unexpected turns of thought, whatever the subject.

* * * *

Donne's first religious sonnets, "La Corona," a sequence that everyone agrees is unusually impersonal for Donne, are generally dated to about 1608, when his friendship with Lady Bedford was developing.

These seven sonnets, linked into a single poem or "corona" by the device of repeating the last line of each sonnet as the first of its successor, take their materials, as Gardner and Martz pointed out, from liturgical and devotional tradition.[5] After an introductory sonnet that Gardner relates to the Advent liturgies, there are six sonnets on theological mysteries related to the life of Christ, and each sonnet plays upon paradoxes traditionally associated with its mystery: that Mary's son is her brother and father ("Annunciation"), that the baby in the stable is the God who made the world ("Nativitie"), that the child Jesus refutes the wisdom he himself taught the temple doctors ("Temple"), that the crucifiers "prescribe a Fate" to him who made fate ("Crucifying"), and that Christ's death defeats death ("Resurrection" and "Ascension"). Martz thought that, like Southwell's sequence of fourteen poems on Mary and Jesus, Donne's seven sonnets were based on a version of the Rosary called "the Corona of Our Lady." Yet neither sequence has more than a very general relationship to the Rosary; as Joseph Scallon pointed out (97) in connection with the Southwell set, "no-one has yet shown that there ever existed a form of the Rosary which included exactly those mysteries which Southwell has written about" And the same is true of "La Corona".[6]

It is altogether more probable that Donne's approach was based on Southwell's, whose poems were popular and well-known. Although Southwell's sequence was never printed as a whole in Donne's lifetime, it was easily accessible in the manuscripts circulating circa 1595–1610. In "La Corona," Donne can strike exactly the note of elevated plainness that distinguishes Southwell's poems. Nonetheless, related as the two sets of poems are, their effects are different. Southwell's sequence makes the stronger effect because the poems are focused entirely on their materials. They are not about their author; Southwell has framed his sequence with poems on the conception and assumption of the Virgin, Donne with first-person sonnets. The first-person speaker's state of mind, moreover, is problematic:

> *Deigne at my hands this crown of prayer and praise,*
> Weav'd in my low devout melancholie,
> Thou which of good, hast, yea art treasury,
> All changing unchang'd Antient of dayes,
> But doe not, with a vile crowne of fraile bayes,
> Reward my muses white sincerity,
> But what thy thorny crowne gain'd, that give mee,
> A crowne of Glory, which doth flower alwayes;

That "Low devout melancholie" is a puzzle. As Gardner points out: "In general Donne regards melancholy as not conducive to true devotion, but as its enemy. . . 'Low' may mean 'humble'; but Donne usually employs the word in a derogatory sense."[7] Calling a "low melancholy" "devout" may, as Oliver says, give it a "spiritual flavor" but hardly explains why it is the source of a set of contemplative sonnets.[8] Consequently, although a critic such as Lewalski is right to draw attention to Donne's cleverness in ringing the changes on his various "crowns," Donne undercuts his effect by worrying that the divine critic might reward his sincerity with the "vile" consolation prize of poetic glory instead of the real prize of Christian glory—a laurel crown instead of a heavenly crown.

Surely, though, Donne does not expect us to think that salvation might hang upon a set of poems? Or that what Christ gained by suffering others will achieve by sincerity? Or that the author of so ingeniously crafted a set of poems really means it when he expresses contempt for the poet's "vile" art? No resolution of these puzzlements appears in the sestet that follows. Instead, there are four lines of intense verbal conjuring:

> The ends crowne our workes, but thou crown'st our ends,
> For, at our end begins our endlesse rest,
> The first last end, now zealously possest,
> With a strong sober thirst, my soule attends.

This is "conjuring" because the lines deploy a kind of prestidigitation on "ends" and "crown" intended to subsume all ends, including Donne's own, in one transcendant, culminating end. After so much exuberance, "Sober" seems meant to convince us that after a shaky beginning, the poet has a firm grip on religious hope: the "first last end" of all things, including Donne's own life, is the Incarnation, the point in which all history, human and divine, finds its purpose. Therefore:

> 'Tis time that heart and voice be lifted high,
> *Salvation to all that will is nigh.*

This conclusion, referring to passages from the Advent liturgies,[9] suggests that the "turn" or *volta* of the sonnet models a shift from ordinary to liturgical time. The injunction to lift up heart and voice paraphrases the salutation in the preface to the Canon of the Mass: "Lift up your hearts." The last line, too (sometimes read as an anti-Calvinist slogan), is a liturgical rather than a theological statement, an invitation to participation and belief , not a statement of fact. The sequence of sonnets that follows, therefore, is a kind of private liturgical devotion, and its climax comes, like that of the Mass to which it is related, in the sonnets on the Crucifixion and Resurrection. The implication of this form is that "La Corona" is a spiritual as well as a poetic work, offered to Christ as an oblation in the words of its first and last lines: *"Deigne at my hands this crowne of prayer and praise."*[10]

Does the sequence work as a liturgically conceived devotion? One can't help noticing that Donne has reached the impressive conclusion of the first sonnet by verbal play; puns have carried him into the liturgical mode, in which he contemplates divine immensity "cloystered" in the Virgin's womb and instructs his soul to kiss the Christ child ("Nativitie"). When the sequence arrives at the Crucifixion, though, the time-bound first-person voice returns, and with it the conviction that no works, poetic or otherwise, can prevail against death. Only free, unearned, unmerited grace can do that, and the speaker begs the crucified: *"Moyst with one drop of thy blood, my dry soule."* Impelled by that prayer, the final sonnet, "Ascension," reverses the movement of the first and, passing from liturgical time back into ordinary time, returns the speaker to the condition in which he and the sequence began:

> *Salute the last and everlasting day,*
> Joy at the uprising of this Sunne, and Sonne,
> Yee whose just teares, or tribulation
> Have purely washt, or burnt away your drossie clay;
> Behold the Highest, parting hence away,
> Lightens the darke clouds, which hee treads upon,

Nor doth hee by ascending, show alone,
But first hee, and hee first enters the way.
O strong Ramme, which hast batter'd heaven for mee,
Mild lambe, which with thy blood, hast mark'd the path;
Bright torch, which shin'st, that I the way may see,
Oh, with thine owne blood quench thine owne just wrath,
And if thy holy Spirit, my Muse did raise,
Deigne at my hands this crowne of prayer and praise.

Again, the *volta* marks the turn of the mode. That ram, lamb, and torch may be characteristically, even conventionally baroque images,[11] but they are the first of their kind to appear in this poem. With them, and with the worried conditional form of the thirteenth line, the sequence comes full circle back to the melancholy speaker who began it. He is still uncertain of his motives, still doubtful whether motive and intention have any place in the scheme of salvation at all.

"La Corona" is a charming, clever, but inconclusive poem, which shows neither "praise" (in the form of contemplation of religious mystery) nor "prayer" (in the form of direct petition for saving grace) working decisively either for speaker or reader. Indeed, as the analyses of Martz and Lewalski show in their opposed ways, the rewards of reading the poem are more aesthetic than religious; it is meant to arouse delight and admiration among well-educated readers who would appreciate the range of its material (drawn from both Catholic and Protestant sources) and admire its author's unsectarian willingness to refrain from drawing hard conclusions or pressing unfashionable enthusiasms—the treatment of the Blessed Virgin, for instance, manages to be simultaneously Catholic and tactful, something not at all easy to achieve among Protestants in 1608. "La Corona," in fact, is very tasteful, uncharacteristically so for Donne, which suggests that it may have been written for a female patron with fashionable but not overly demanding religious interests.[12] What "La Corona" is not, in any real sense of the word, is a meditative poem. Meditation, as practiced in Donne's time, was a method of contemplative prayer designed to integrate the personality in preparation for Christian action in the form of the *Imitatio Christi*;[13] "La Corona" reveals no such intention.

* * * *

By Helen Gardner's dating, still generally accepted, the first twelve Holy Sonnets proper were written in 1609. Four more followed circa

1610–11. The three sonnets found only in the Westmoreland manuscript were probably written after his ordination, though this dating is
not absolutely certain.[14]

The order is problematic. On the basis of the textual and internal
evidence she used to date them, Gardner established the order found
in her edition, which is followed here (with Patrides' numbers in paren-
thesis); but, persuasive though it is, Gardner's order, like her dates, is
not certain enough to be taken as evidence of Donne's intentions—
and this is true of any ordering of the sonnets, whether found in the
manuscripts or in either of the two early editions (1633, 1635).

The theme of the first six sonnets is death and judgment; the second
six are on the equally difficult, related topics of salvation and the
atonement. If, as seems likely, the sonnet "To the E[arl] of D[orset]
with six holy Sonnets"[15] refers to the first six, it provides a strong hint
of the social context in which Donne wrote them:

> See Sir, how as the Suns hot Masculine flame
> > Begets strange creatures on Niles durty slime,
> > In me, your fatherly yet lusty Ryme
> (For, these songs are their fruits) have wrought the same;
> But though the ingendring force from whence they came
> > Bee strong enough, and nature doe admit
> > Seaven to be borne at once, I send as yet
> But six, they say, the seaventh hath still some maime;
> > I choose your judgement, which the same degree
> > Doth with her sister, your invention, hold,
> As fire these drossie Rymes to purifie,
> > Or as Elixir, to change them to gold;
> You are that Alchimist which alwaies had
> Wit, whose one spark could make good things of bad.
> > > > > > > > > > (*Poems,* 294)

The Holy Sonnets, then, were written for a male audience and, complimentary though it is, the Dorset sonnet has an aggressively competitive tone. Responding to Dorset's efforts, Donne has produced "seven
at a birth"; and though the seventh "hath still some maime," the six
he is sending are strong enough to withstand criticism. What Dorset
will be looking for—he of the fiery, refining judgment—is wit and invention.

Since Donne confesses that Dorset's poems were his incentive, and
since he gives his poems to Dorset unreservedly as objects upon

which to exercise his wit, we should be wary of assuming that the sonnets are a variety of autobiography. The "strong" subjects—death and
judgment, atonement, grace, and salvation—in which romantically
conditioned readers have found indications of Donne's state of mind[16]
when he wrote are just as likely to be the kind of religious subject men
like Donne and Dorset thought suitable for "the hot masculine flame"
of their invention and wit.

The autobiography of Sir Toby Mathew, converted to Catholicism
in 1606, throws a biographical sidelight on the period when Donne
was writing the Holy Sonnets. In 1607, when Mathew returned from
Italy as a Catholic, the authorities imprisoned him. His friends, including Donne, visited him. They talked religion, and Mathew concluded
that Donne and another friend, Martin, "were mere libertines in themselves":

> The thing for which they could not long endure me was because they
> thought me too saucy, for presuming to show them the right way, in which
> they liked not then to go, and wherein they would disdain to follow any
> other.[17]

In calling Donne a libertine, Mathew was not accusing him of immo-
rality or atheism; he was describing him as an ecclesiastical free-
thinker, unwilling to commit himself. Other biographical indications of
the period support Mathew. In 1607/08 Donne wrote *Biathanatos*, a
work calculated to shock had it ever been published. As late as 1611,
besides writing *Ignatius his Conclave*, he was still revising his *Courtier's
Library*, a witty little book that jokes about Catholics and Protestants
indifferently.[18] Features of the Holy Sonnets that seem out of place in
poetic meditation (ambiguous theology, bravado, readiness to surprise and shock) are not so surprising in sonnets written by a free-
thinking wit for male readers. The best of them are remarkably clever,
accomplished poems. Like Sidney, Donne chose the difficult, rhyme-
hungry Italian form of the sonnet. In the octave, he invariably used
two closed quatrains, rhyming ABBA/ABBA. For the sestet, he used
three rhymes arranged in a quatrain followed by a couplet, and in all
but four of the nineteen Holy Sonnets the couplet is syntactically inte-
grated with the sestet. The result of this demanding form is a tightly
packed, economical composition, written mostly in a plain, energetic
style. A soliloquizing voice caught in a moment of conflict argues
strong, difficult subjects; style and mode of self-presentation reveal
the influence of the theater.

Perhaps because of their dramatic quality, the sonnets can be surprisingly insubstantial, even unstable. Here is the octave of Sonnet 1
(2):

> As due by many titles I resigne
> My selfe to thee, O God, first I was made
> By thee, and for thee, and when I was decay'd
> Thy blood bought that, the which before was thine,
> I am thy sonne, made with thy selfe to shine,
> Thy servant, whose paines thou hast still repaid,
> Thy sheepe, thine Image, and till I betray'd
> My selfe, a temple of thy Spirit divine;

That *sounds* like impulsive prayer. There is an act of resignation in the
present moment, a making-over of the self to God to whom it belongs
because He made it and bought it; it's his son, his servant, his sheep,
his image, and finally a temple for His divine spirit. Then, with the
sestet, come the questions: "Why doth the devill then usurpe in
mee? / Why doth he steale, nay ravish that's thy right?" Since the
speaker has already confessed to betraying himself, one would think
the answer fairly obvious; but no, using an image Donne and his
friends evidently enjoyed, the speaker insists he is the victim of down-
right rape, and tells his divine owner that unless He puts up a fight for
His property, it will be lost:

> Except thou rise and for thine owne worke fight,
> Oh I shall soone despaire, when I doe see
> That thou lov'st mankind well, yet wilt'not chuse me,
> And Satan hates mee, yet is loth to lose mee.

That resolution on a double rhyme could sound rather flippant. And
perhaps it is: if the devil has really ravished the speaker, then the pro-
posed act of resignation cannot take place because the self, however
due to God it may be, belongs at this moment to the usurping devil.
In fact, the real peculiarity of this sonnet is that nothing at all happens
in it despite its urgent opening; there is no resignation, no rising and
fighting, and no despairing. The whole statement is conditional on the
opening, "As due by many titles": if the law has any force, that is, then
certain things follow; but Satan's usurpation has overturned the speaker's ability to follow the law, and so he constructs a neat box of witty
doctrine to contain a hypothetically emergent, but in fact absent, self,

lost between self-betrayal and/or rape, and a remaking that so far shows no signs of happening. God doesn't choose him, and Satan doesn't lose him, but in the meantime he fills the present void with a well-wrought sonnet on an unstated theme: "O God, make me good, but not yet."

A similar instability appears in the second sonnet. Donne never wrote a love poem on the basis of a hypothesis—for example, "Imagine that you are in bed with a girl. What would you think? What would you feel?" But this is how he writes Holy Sonnet 2 (4) on sin and repentance: "Oh my blacke Soule! now thou art summoned / By sicknesse, deaths herald, and champion." Now whether Donne wrote thus because he and his friends agreed that the proof of all theological puddings will come at the moment of death or because, as Louis Martz and his followers aver, this was St. Ignatius Loyala's recommended way of writing poems, the difference between writing about what has been and what might be is the difference between experience and pretense. Why, one wonders, is the unfortunate soul black? What has it done? "Black" is as evasive as it's melodramatic, but two succeeding images hint at the soul's plight. Firstly, it is like a pilgrim who, having committed treason abroad, does not want to come home, and secondly it is like a thief on the way to execution who wishes he were back in prison. These images suggest dark, even brutal comedy. The soul so imagined is more shifty than defiant; those crimes, in the context of eternity, are no great matter, may not even be crimes at all. They are certainly not the criminal equivalent of mortal sin. In the world where those images originated, it was the state that condemned felons and brought people home for trial, sometimes by kidnapping them. Moreover, people accused of treason abroad and brought home for trial tended to be Catholics. If Dennis Flynn is right about Donne's activities as a young Catholic, Donne could have found himself in just such a plight.[19] This sonnet is not saying all it might about the circumstances of its speaker.

In any case, if sickness, death's champion, is challenging this soul to fight, the soul will not prove much of a fighter—but then, one wonders, what is the fight about? The undeveloped implication is that the body is the soul's prison or home in exile, and, given its circumstances, the soul might well put up a fight to stay there rather than be sent back where it belongs. In fact, one can imagine a different outcome to the poem in which that troubled soul was given something to say for itself—about forced repatriation, for instance.

In the sestet, the authoritative voice that told the black soul to imagine itself summoned by sickness tells it that although repentance will
bring grace, the real difficulty is to acquire the grace that makes repentance possible in the first place. Caught in that impasse, the soul is
then told to make itself as black with mourning and red with blushing
as it is red and black with sin or, alternatively, to wash itself in Christ's
blood, which dyes red souls white. So a condition that begins with
metaphor is cured with metaphor, while the unfortunate felons of the
simile continue on their way to execution. What is the soul actually
being told to do? Feel sorry for itself and go to confession or communion? Be born again? The most interesting things in this sonnet are the
soul's hopeless position, and the strong, though occluded, complex of
feeling locked up in the image of the unwilling prisoner haled to execution.

Donne's readiness to surprise, and to flirt with the impermissible,
continually sets problems of tone for his reader and, one suspects,
often led him towards subjects he could not treat openly in poems
written for the fashionable and powerful. Like its predecessors, Sonnet
3 (6) hypothesizes the moment of death, this time in frankly theatrical
terms: "This is my playes last scene." Again, the fear of death itself,
rather than its theological trappings, is the sonnet's subject, expressed
in a violent, shocking image:

> And gluttonous death, will instantly unjoynt
> My body, and soule, and I shall sleepe a space,
> But my'ever-waking part shall see that face,
> Whose feare already shakes my every joynt:

The repeated rhyme on "joynt," closing the quatrain, has the sinis-
ter effect of implying that "gluttonous death" and "that face" might
amount to the same thing as far as the feelings are concerned, since
the one shakes the joints and the other unjoints them: Donne's God
can terrify too, but the theological sestet of the sonnet evades that
terror with a slogan:

> Impute me righteous, thus purg'd of evill,
> For thus I leave the world, the flesh, the devill.

It is hard to know how seriously to take that, since from a strictly Protestant point of view the imputation of righteousness, something of a

party rallying cry, was not to be prayed for, let alone demanded;[20] but whether serious or not, the effect of the couplet, following upon the horrors of the octave, is something like, "Just take care of me; that's all that matters." At such moments the poet's aim is not so much to declare an allegiance, as by hook or by crook to find a space for the frightened soul in the theological pandemonium.

Things come clearer in Sonnet 4 (7), with its miniature epic scene of the souls summoned to the sight of God by the angels' trumpets. For once, Donne is not part of the scene he has imagined; his sin excludes him. In the sestet, therefore, he prays God to delay Judgment, and "here on this lowly ground, / Teach mee how to repent." Coming after the other sonnets, this modest request is surprising. Except for "lowly ground," there is no imagery at all; instead there is a confession of something the previous sonnets have implied, that the speaker cannot repent because he does not know how to. And there, perhaps, was Donne's religious problem in a nutshell.

Death obsesses the speaker of these sonnets, threatening final dissolution of the thinking, feeling self, and exclusion from the happy community of the accepted. Fear of death is the defining symptom of his sinfulness, so much so that he does not otherwise seem to *feel* sinful at all. He shows no interest in the details of his sins. He can even protest the whole scheme of salvation and damnation, as in the octave of sonnet 5 (9):

> If poysonous mineralls, and if that tree,
> Whose fruit threw death on else immortall us,
> If lecherous goats, if serpents envious
> Cannot be damn'd; Alas; why should I bee?

Nor does he have an answer to his question, except, "But who am I, that dare dispute with thee?," which allies him with the exemplary Job.[21] Yet the question is his own, and deserves an answer.[22] The most surprising demonstration of Donne's uninterest in the particularities of his sins, and of his readiness to use any sophistry to trick death's door-keeper, appears in the sestet of Sonnet 9. The speaker, imagining himself on the verge of death, tells his soul to look in his heart for the remembered (and *very* Catholic) picture of the crucified Christ:

> Teares in his eyes quench the amasing light,
> Blood fills his frownes, which from his pierc'd head fell,

> And can that tongue adjudge thee unto hell,
> Which pray'd forgivenesse for his foes fierce spight?

The sestet's answer is "No, no;"

> but as in my idolatrie
> I said to all my profane mistresses,
> Beauty, of pitty, foulnesse onely is
> A signe of rigour: so I say to thee,
> To wicked spirits are horrid shapes assign'd,
> This beauteous forme assumes a pitious minde.

Coming on the heels of the description of the crucifix, that use of "idolatrie" is outrageous.[23] As Donne knew, to the Protestant English mind, idolatry expressed itself in the adoration of things like crucifixes, not girls. For people in the know, moreover, Donne's own idolatry had consisted of Catholicism, not womanizing. But Donne's cheekiness is only beginning. The proposition that an argument he once used to get into bed with pretty girls will now get him into heaven with a beautiful God may have amused the earl of Dorset, but it would have offended Christians of all sects.[24]

Of the first twelve sonnets, probably the most admired is number 10 (14), "Batter my heart," in which Donne develops more completely the imagery of usurpation and rape deployed in Sonnet 1. This time, the *volta* or "turn" between octave and sestet, a marked feature of its predecessors, which has consistently marked the gulf to be crossed between heaven and earth or sin and salvation, is hardly felt at all, swept away as it is in the imagining of an extraordinarily violent act against the self. Look, says the speaker to God, I am a prisoner, unwillingly betrothed to your enemy. I am an enslaved, occupied city, unfree to act either for good or evil. Take me by force, invade me, imprison me, rape me; I shall never be free or chaste otherwise.[25]

The sonnet is so thoroughly worked out, so confident in its exuberant violence, that readers have had difficulty relating it to anything outside of itself, as if, considered as extended metaphor, it is all vehicle and no tenor. Students have looked for similar sonnets; they have quarried the emblem books for similar images, and they have squabbled over its theology, but they have seldom asked, What is it about? What is Donne asking for, and why? In the world of ordinary religious psychology, Donne would be asking, if in extravagant terms, for a con-

version experience, for the sort of thing that still happens in evangeli-
cal churches. Yet since nothing we know about Donne suggests he
would have welcomed such an experience, this sonnet's events, like
those of its predecessors, belong to the imagined time of death and
judgment. The condition the speaker aspires to reach by annihilation
is ineffable; he knows nothing about it at firsthand. What he does know
about is the unsatisfactory present moment; and since he has been a
soldier and a womanizer in his time, he knows about the means he
urges upon God: he is familiar with war and rape, with sieges and se-
ductions.

As with some of the other sonnets, read as theology this imagery
has a mischievous effect. Donne is asking for the rule of reason and
love to be restored, but as an answer to that longing, it is hard to take
seriously either his violent God or the theology that requires him to
act that way. One might even argue that Calvinist anti-intellectualism,
having dethroned reason, required a God like this: this sonnet's God,
like the God of Sonnets 3 and 5, is implicated in the problem. On the
other hand, the human implication of the sonnet's imagery is that to
people in despair over the world's irrationality, violence can be liberat-
ing and defining, a defense of the unsecured, abandoned self against
religious uncertainty and the fear of death—a proposition shortly to
be tested in action by Donne's fellow Europeans in the Thirty Years'
War, and by his fellow English in their own civil wars.[26]

Although "Batter my heart" is the most admired of the sonnets, the
most popular is probably number 6 (10), "Death be not proud." It too
is based on a paradox, that death will die; and while it is true that the
paradox expresses common Christian belief, the ground bass of all
these sonnets is a conviction that mere belief or knowledge gives no
protection against the unreason of death and judgment. The sonnets'
purpose is to provide a kind of technology for taming terror by enact-
ing the thing feared, eloquently, argumentatively, and wittily: the
poetry aims to control the grounds of fear by objectifying them in artful, ceremonious verbal form. In a word, Donne's art draws on a kind
of magical thinking.[27] Sonnet 6 is an incantation, spoken against a figure mostly of the poet's own invention—Death as bogus lord, mock
ruler, and jumped-up servant of a greater master than himself—and
culminating in the final line's enunciation of a visionary order beyond
time as we know it: "And death shall be no more, death, thou shalt
die."

Logically, of course, it's an irrational proposition. Death's nonbeing is another aspect of the ineffable, amenable only to sophistical reasoning. Death as braggart and bully, "slave to Fate, chance, kings, and desperate men," is a straw man, the invention of a high-spirited masculine stoicism accustomed to negotiating a position for itself in a world of violent, arbitrary power. As with the other sonnets, nothing actually happens in it; the event it proposes to shape or coerce will take place in eschatological time, and as is often the case, one feels that much that's on the author's mind is not being said—on the subject of the "kings" mentioned in line 9, for instance. Moreover, as the imagery of Sonnet 10 revisits themes in Sonnet 1, so this poem's strongest, most developed image of death's work picks up a motif from Sonnet 2:

> And soonest our best men with thee doe goe,
> Rest of their bones, and soules deliverie.

"Soules deliverie" is a variant of "gaol-delivery," that melancholy ritual by which Jacobean justice delivered up its prisoners to trial and execution. Thinking of Death's depredations, Donne's mind is back with the unfortunates of Sonnet 2, whose fate no amount of witty incantation could charm away. Whom he was thinking of? What names occurred to the men who first read this poem?

The plight of the solitary soul among contested theologies preoccupies the writer of the Holy Sonnets, which throw an oblique, sometimes ghastly light on the crises of conscience, the terror of death, and the dread of personal annihilation that ignited the religious wars of the seventeenth century. In principle Donne, who knew what was at stake, probably had intimations of what was coming and what was needed to forestall it: "Thy lawes abridgement, and thy last command," Sonnet 12 (16) concludes, "Is all but love; Oh let this last Will stand!" Donne seems never to have reneged, despite his advancement as courtly Dean, on the insight of Satire III, that the division of Christendom was its tragedy, that it was deeply irrational, and that it left anyone capable of thought profoundly isolated from the enthusiasms of the times. Donne's maneuvering between Catholic and Protestant positions, his cheeky deployment of the weaponry of either side, and his witty evasions are traceable to that understanding.

He returned to the subject in what may be the last of his sonnets, "Show me deare Christ," which Gardner dated 1620, at the beginning of the Thirty Years' War, after the Protestant defeat at the Battle of the White Mountain, 29 October 1620:

> Show me deare Christ, thy Spouse, so bright and clear.
> What! is it she, which on the other shore
> Goes richly painted? or which rob'd and tore
> Laments and mournes in Germany and here?
> Sleepes she a thousand, then peepes up one yeare?
> Is she selfe truth and errs? now new, now outwore?
> Doth she, and did she, and shall she evermore
> On one, on seaven, or on no hill appeare?
> Dwells she with us, or like adventuring knights
> First travaile we to seeke and then make Love?
> Betray kind husband thy spouse to our sights,
> And let myne amorous soule court thy mild Dove,
> Who is most trew, and pleasing to thee, then
> When she'is embrac'd and open to most men.

Scholars, having agreed to be shocked by the concluding image of this sonnet, have devoted most of their energies to debating whether Donne could have written it in good faith and remained an ordained member of the Church of England. Yet this final eruption of Donne's imagination in sonnet form delivers a judgment quite separate from the subsidiary question: which, if any, contemporary church is the true one? Donne's verdict on the religious error of his times is in the shock of the last line: the true church, by definition, is open to all, and that is why nobody wants it. And there is a further, sharply satirical, even despairing implication: the men of Europe are as likely to join in communion with the bride of Christ as they are to share their women.

The older Yeats wondered whether lines of his had sent young men to war in Ireland. One can imagine Donne's sonnet distressing and enraging some contemporary readers. Although it was unpublished until Edmund Gosse printed it in 1899, it circulated in manuscript. One wonders: in 1642 did some puritan, or cavalier read or remember that sonnet and saying to himself, "Not if I have anything to say about it," buckle his armor?

NOTES

1. R. C. Bald, *John Donne, a Life* (New York: Oxford University Press, 1970), 161.
2. Isaak Walton, *The Lives* (1927; rpt. London: Oxford University Press, 1973), 48.

3. Dennis Flynn, *John Donne and the Ancient Catholic Nobility* (Bloomington: Indiana University Press). See also Donne's poem, "To Mr. Tilman after he had taken orders," and Helen Gardner's comment upon it in *John Donne: The Divine Poems* (Oxford: Clarendon, 1978), 127–32.

4. E.g., "Donne wrote most of his religious poetry as a preparation for taking holy orders." Mary Ann Radzinowicz, "Anima Mea' Psalms and John Donne's Religious Poetry," in *"Bright Shootes of Everlastingness": The Seventeenth-Century Religious Lyric,* ed. Claude J. Summers and Ted-Larry Pebworth (Columbia: University of Missouri Press, 1987), 43.

5. Gardner, *John Donne,* xxi–xxiv; Louis L. Martz, *The Poetry of Meditation,* rev. ed. (New Haven: Yale University Press), 107–12.

6. For Southwell's poems, see James D. McDonald and Nancy Pollard Brown, eds., *The Poems of Robert Southwell* (Oxford: Clarendon, 1967).

7. Gardner, *John Donne,* 58.

8. P. M. Oliver, *Donne's Religious Writing: A Discourse of Feigned Devotion* (London: Addison Wesley Longman, 1977), 99.

9. Gardner, *John Donne,* 57–58.

10. "Though intended for private use, the Corona sonnets are close to public discipline and communion of feeling . . . [they] are not, of course, literally hymn or song texts, but they share the pronounced vocal and liturgical qualities of these forms." Anthony Low, *Love's Architecture: Devotional Modes in Seventeenth-Century Poetry* (New York: New York University Press, 1978), 51.

11. Barbara Lewalski, *Protestant Poetics and the Seventeenth-Century Religious Lyric* (Princeton: Princeton University Press, 1979), 202.

12. Touches of sentimentality (e.g., 3.1, *"deare wombe";* 3.13, "Kisse him, and with him into Egypt goe, / With his kinde mother, who partakes thy woe"; and 6.8, the "little booke" of life that so puzzled Gardner) as well as the melancholy of its presenting speaker, both noticed by Oliver (*Donne's Religious Writing,* 99, 103) suggest a female audience. It seems unlikely, though, that the poem corresponds to the "hymns" Donne describes in a dedicatory sonnet to Magdalen Herbert, which Gardner printed as preface to the sequence. Walton, who ought to have known, said that Mrs. Herbert's "hymns" were lost.

13. Anthony D. Cousins, *The Catholic Religious Poets from Southwell to Crashaw* (London: Sheed and Ward, 1991), 30–37.

14. Gardner, *John Donne,* xxxvii–lv, 57, 65, 75, 77–78, 151–52.

15. Gardner, following Grierson, identifies "E. of D" as Richard Sackville, 3rd earl of Dorset, who succeeded to the title 28 September 1609 following the death of his father, Robert, the 2nd earl, on 27 February 1609.

16. "The note of anguish is unmistakable. The image of a soul in meditation which the 'Holy Sonnets' present is an image of a soul working out its salvation in fear and trembling" (Gardner, *John Donne,* xxxi).

17. Bald, *John Donne, a Life,* 188.

18. Bald, *John Donne, a Life,* 201, 241; Oliver, *Donne's Religious Writing,* 133–34.

19. Flynn, *John Donne and the Ancient Catholic Nobility,* 131–46, argues that, having gone to Paris with the earl of Derby's embassy in 1585, young John Donne was present with other English exiles at the prince of Parma's siege of Antwerp.

20. Oliver, *Donne's Religious Writing,* 120–22.

21. See Job 42.2–4; also Lewalski, *Protestant Poetics;* 269.

22. Not everyone agrees. "An audacious, blasphemous evasion of responsibility"

(Martz, *Poetry of Meditation,* 52); "frantic ravings" (Low, *Love's Architecture,* 65); "a specious argument" (Lewalski, *Protestant Poetics,* 269). What is going on here? Donne's question seems reasonable enough; see Oliver's comment: "This is one of the rare moments in the *Holy Sonnets* when one feels that Donne's 'I' and 'me' are representative pronouns: his speaker stands for a generation of souls painfully conscious of their sinfulness and yet unwilling to accept that a loving God can be so cruel as to have arbitrarily damned them before they even possessed the option of sinning. . . . It's the closest any speaker of the *Holy Sonnets* comes to asking his creator why he created him" (*Donne's Religious Writing,* 124–25).

23. "The very slyness of these lines is troubling. . . . The manipulative insincerity of the erotic analogy, however, infects his expression of desire for Christ" (R. V. Young, "Donne's *Holy Sonnets* and the Theology of Grace," in *"Bright Shootes of Everlastingness,"* ed. Summers and Pebworth, 35–36).

24. To the average reader, this sonnet's strangest feature is the description of the baroque crucifix as beautiful, and its association with women's beauty, an extravagance that leads Oliver to suspect that "if the poem draws on the *Spiritual Exercises* at all, is does so in a spirit close to that of parody." He may be right. A similar juxtaposition of a crucifix and women's beauty appears in Southwell's *Epistle of Comfort* (1587: 35a–38b), arguing that to imitate Christ truly we must understand that beauty, hence the true object of love, is to be found in the crucified Christ, and not in women. Donne's sonnet stands Southwell's argument on its head; anyone who knew/knows the Southwell passage will see that the sonnet travesties it.

25. Whether Donne, who according to Christopher Ricks resented even his own orgasms, would have welcomed rape in any form, metaphorical or not, is doubtful: "Donne's poems, whether or not they are personal memories, record a dislike of having come" (Ricks, "John Donne: 'Farewell to Love,'" in *Essays in Appreciation* [Oxford: Clarendon, 1996], 19).

26. Frank Warnke's comment, in *John Donne* (Boston: Twayne, 1987), 110, shows how adroitly criticism elides the violence of the poem: "The dazzling paradoxes of the conclusion reaffirm the degree to which Donne was an artist of the baroque—not only in his reckless extravagance of technique but also in his deep conviction that, in a world where all is illusion, divine truth inevitably presents itself in terms that seem absurd or self-contradictory to earthly wisdoms." Donne's technique is disciplined, not recklessly extravagant, and the poem's violence is emotionally felt.

27. Kirby Farrell examines Shakespeare's Sonnets as magical thinking, commenting on Sonnet 105: "The enacted sonnet conceives a mysterious root integrity beyond the lifeless or promiscuous meanings words have in ordinary use . . . such a root meaning confutes the world of apparent change, the rational world under the sway of death." Farrell, *Shakespeare's Creation: The Language of Magic and Play* (Amherst: University of Massachusetts Press, 1995). Farrell's analysis is relevant to Donne's technique in the Holy Sonnets, especially his dependence upon pun and paradox.

WORKS CITED

Bald, R. C. *John Donne, a Life.* New York: Oxford University Press, 1970.

Cousins, Anthony D. *The Catholic Religious Poets from Southwell to Crashaw.* London: Sheed and Ward, 1991.

Farrell, Kirby. *Shakespeare's Creation: The Language of Magic and Play.* Amherst: University of Massachusetts Press, 1975.

Flynn, Dennis. *John Donne and the Ancient Catholic Nobility.* Bloomington: Indiana University Press, 1995.

Gardner, Helen, ed. *John Donne: The Divine Poems.* Oxford: Clarendon, 1978.

Lewalski, Barbara. *Protestant Poetics and the Seventeenth-Century Religious Lyric.* Princeton: Princeton University Press, 1979.

Low, Anthony. *Love's Architecture: Devotional Modes in Seventeenth-Century Poetry.* New York: New York University Press, 1978.

Martz, Louis L. *The Poetry of Meditation.* Rev. ed. New Haven: Yale University Press, 1962.

McDonald, James D., and Nancy Pollard Brown, eds. *The Poems of Robert Southwell, S.J.* Oxford: Clarendon Press, 1967.

Oliver, P. M. *Donne's Religious Writing: A Discourse of Feigned Devotion.* London: Addison Wesley Longman, 1997.

Radzinowicz, Mary Ann. " 'Anima Mea' Psalms and John Donne's Religious Poetry." In *"Bright Shootes of Everlastingnesse": The Seventeenth-Century Religious Lyric,* edited by Claude J. Summers and Ted-Larry Pebworth. Columbia: University Press of Missouri, 1987.

Ricks, Christopher. "John Donne: 'Farewell to Love'." In *Essays in Appreciation.* Oxford: Clarendon, 1996.

Scallon, Joseph D. *The Poetry of Robert Southwell, S.J.* Salzburg: Institut für Englische Sprache und Literatur, 1975.

Walton, Isaak. *The Lives.* 1927; rpt. London: Oxford University Press, 1973.

Warnke, Frank J. *John Donne.* Boston: Twayne, 1987.

Young, R. V. "Donne's *Holy Sonnets* and the Theology of Grace." In *"Bright Shootes of Everlastingnesse": The Seventeenth-Century Religious Lyric,* edited by Claude J. Summers and Ted-Larry Pebworth. Columbia: University of Missouri Press, 1987.

Gender, Genre, and the Idea of John Donne in the *Anniversaries*

MAREA MITCHELL

> Immortal Mayd, who though thou wouldst refuse
> The name of Mother, be unto my Muse,
> A Father, since her chaste Ambition is,
> Yearly to bring forth such a child as this.
> —"The Second Anniversary," 33–36.

REACTING TO CRITICISM OF HIS POEMS COMMEMORATING THE DEATH OF fifteen-year-old Elizabeth Drury, Donne famously remarked that he wrote not about the girl herself but about "The Idea of a woman and not as she was."[1] Defending himself against charges of the poem's inappropriateness in its hyperbolic praise of a young woman whom he, it seems, had never met, Donne asserted that the reader was to take the part for the whole, that Elizabeth Drury was to be seen as in some senses metonymical: "I would not be thought to have gone about to praise her, or any other in rime; except I took such a person, as might be capable of all I could say."[2] As has been remarked from a different perspective, "to read the poems written in praise of Elizabeth Drury is to be forced to forget Elizabeth Drury in order to remember Donne."[3]

In some ways, Donne's statements are part of a tradition, well-marked and criticized by feminism, in which the female body and character are both completely insignificant and vitally important. In herself, as an individual woman, Elizabeth Drury is so unimportant as to never be mentioned by name at all within the two poems that owe their existence to her. Like loyal companions in spaghetti westerns who die en route to the film's denouement, Drury's purpose is fulfilled in her death. As Joseph Hall put it, rather more starkly and less diplomatically than Donne himself, Drury was fortunate in the timing of her death.[4] Luckily for her, Donne was around to write about it. She, "Thrise noble maid," became immortal through virtue of the poet's

106

writing and, as Hall wrote of her, "couldst not have found nor sought /
A fitter time to yeeld to thy sad Fate, / Than whiles this spirit lives;
that can relate / Thy worth so well to our last nephews eyne."[5]

Yet as vehicle for an anatomy or reflection about the world and
human activity Elizabeth Drury is vitally important. From her death
the poet proffers important insights, perhaps most evident where the
conjunction between Drury's death and Donne's anatomy is signaled
by linguistic formulation and repetition:

> Shee, shee is dead; shee's dead: when thou knowest this,
> Thou knowest how poore a trifling thing man is.
> And learn'st thus much by our Anatomee . . .
>
> Shee, shee is dead, she's dead; when thou knowst this
> Thou knowst how ugly a monster this world is:
> And learnst thus much by our Anatomee . . .
>
> Shee, shee is dead; shee's dead: when thou knowst this,
> Thou knowst how wan a Ghost this our world is:
> And learnst thus much by our Anatomee . . .
>
> Shee, shee is dead; shee's dead; when thou knowst this,
> Thou knowst how drie a Cinder this world is.
> And learnst thus much by our Anatomy . . .
>   ("An Anatomy," 183–85; 325–27; 369–71; 427–29.)

The selection of these passages from the poem, although out of context, emphasizes the effect that they have within the poem. All four
occur after a particularly excessive moment where the dead girl is
compared with things far beyond herself. In the first, she is associated
with virtue and the abolition of the stain of Eve; in the second, she is
seen to be the epitome of proportion and the means by which all civil
war is ended—nominally within the human psyche, but with implications beyond that. In the third, she is the fount of all beauty, color, and
growth; in the fourth, the source of all goodness that could possibly
exist in a postlapsarian world.

While C. S. Lewis was not specific in relation to particular lines in
the *Anniversaries*, it is hard not to have some sympathy with his comments about the "insanity" (79) of various parts of the poems given
the sense of excess that accompanies these lines.[6] In each individual
case, the insistence that the object and subject of the poem is dead

could work as a lament, as an emphasis to bring home to the reader the sense of personal loss. Yet the repetition of the pronoun "she" also falls awkwardly given that the preceding lines have moved far beyond any presumed or suggested reality of the fifteen-year-old girl. The reader is brought back to the occasion for the poem in a way that destabilizes the relationship between occasion and anatomy. The dead body of the girl will not sustain the philosophical weights, is not substantial enough for the hyperbolic flights, that Donne insistently wants it to bear.

This disjunction, the assault on the imagination of the reader that the disparity constitutes and that has been so often remarked, serves another purpose—namely to emphasize the role of the poet in the manufacture of the verse itself. It is not only, or not even, the death of one Elizabeth Drury that illustrates the frivolity or insubstantiality of the world, but Donne's use of it in the anatomy. As many times as Drury's death is flashed in the face of the reader, so too is the invocation that s/he "learnst much by our anatomy." Yet this later clause is subordinated to the repeated "she, she, she," and takes an adjunct status, appearing as a less significant attachment, where the "*And* learnst thus much" suggests itself as corollary rather than purpose. Furthermore, the use of the plural pronoun "our" mitigates the sense of individual purpose or investment on the part of the persona within the poem. As such it directly contrasts with Donne's more forthright, defensive statement concerning his intentions about the poems, where the relationship between poem and subject is more directly articulated: "I took such a person, as might be capable of all I could say."[7] Here Drury is "*taken*" by Donne as the means for an unfolding of everything he is capable of saying, in a way that explicitly relegates her to occasion rather than subject. The "our" within the poem camouflages the purposes of the controlling author's "I."

The paradox of the centrality and peripheral nature of Woman and Elizabeth Drury is directly approached in "A Funerall Elegie." Here, any person who would "true good prefer" becomes Drury's representative, her replacement on earth.

> Every such person is her delegate,
>   T'accomplish that which should have beene her fate.
> They shall make up that booke, and shall have thankes
>   Of fate and her, for filling up their blanks.

>   (99–102)

Drury, cut short from the life that should have been hers, then lives vicariously in the lives of others who can learn from virtue and the example that she set. She is thus an empty vessel filled by others, and at the same time the means by which they are filled. She is both dead and alive, present and absent, here and gone. Quite literally, she is the means by which the meaning of others is constructed precisely through ceasing to have physical meaning herself.

There are, of course, familiar tropes at work here. The female subject is guaranteed immortality through the poet's verse, an idea made most famously by Shakespeare's Sonnet 18 ("Shall I compare thee to a summer's day?"). There is a suggestion too of the pen/body metaphor so explicitly taken up in Philip Sidney's "No tongue can her perfections tell,/In whose each part all pens may dwell."[8] The familiarity of this image is indicated in Joseph Hall's positing a "mutual grace" between Donne's "cunning pencil" and Drury's "comely face" (in "To the Praise of the Dead," 17, 18). What this masks are the specific inequalities between writer and written, not the least of which are his continued existence as opposed to her extinction, and his continuing fame as opposed to her obscurity.[9]

Yet while many of the individual images used within the poems are familiar or variations on conventional themes, there are also peculiarities that go some way to accounting for the difficulties and discomfort associated with the poems. Particularly, for a modern reader, there are contradictions around the use of the anatomy that are disturbing in their implications, especially in relation to the representation of gender within this particular type of poem and in relation to its position within Donne's oeuvre. While there are distinctions to be made between the so-called first and second anniversaries, there are also connections between the two—in the continuation of themes and imagery associated with human bodies and the anatomy that are begun in the first anniversary, which linger and reappear in the second poem.[10] In many of these occurs a sense of violence arising not only from the imagery itself but also from the juxtaposition of dissimilar ideas, which elsewhere has been seen as such a successful part of Donne's poetry, notably the *Songs and Sonnets*. In the *Anniversaries*, there is a different kind of *discordia concors* evident as much in the violence as in the yoking together of images and ideas. More fundamentally, some of the difficulties of the poems arise from the principles of the anatomy itself, the suppositions it contains about the relationship between poet and subject matter (particularly in terms of gender), and the contradictions to which these relationships give rise given the nature of the poems as elegy and commemoration.

Jonathan Sawday's examination of the anatomy in Renaissance culture identifies the twin icons of *Anatomia*, the mirror and the knife, which contributes to an interpretation of Donne's poems. The act of anatomy has a double function: "dissection is an insistence on the partition of something (or someone) which (or who) hitherto possessed their own organic integrity" and constitutes "an act whereby something can also be constructed, or given a concrete presence."[11] At the literal level of the physical anatomy, the dissection of the dead body by the living physician is for the purpose of constructing a further "body" of knowledge, an understanding of the mechanisms of human beings. For Donne, the death of Elizabeth Drury, the contemplation of the end of her physical existence, of her dead body, gives rise to an anatomy or dissection of the "frailty and decay of this whole world." The Elizabeth Drury who did exist, who possessed her own organic integrity, is dissected in the name of extolling her praises. The elegy and anniversaries that commemorate her take her apart, partition her, to do so. At the same time this is also part of the process of constructing a poetic voice, a means of testing and demonstrating what Donne the poet is capable of saying.

Within the poems the idea of the anatomy is used in a variety of ways that can be linked with the dual aims of dissecting—coming to an understanding through a detailed examination—and constructing, this time of the poetic voice. Both of these functions are variously and contradictorily inflected in relation to gender. Furthermore, intersecting or cross-hatching the image and idea of the anatomy, which is central to the first poem and carried over into the second anniversary, are the twin images of birth and death, manipulated to illuminate both the philosophical musings of the persona as well as to link back to the poems' occasion.

Take, for example, one of the first images of the anatomy. The world, bereft of Drury's presence, languishes in earthquake (11), bleeds in tears (12), is sapped of its vital spirits (13), tormented by consumption and fever (19). Yet it cannot be said that there is no life at all, argues the speaker, as if to account for the obvious contradiction of his own voice speaking, "For there's a kind of world remaining still" (67). This world is animated by the shadow of Drury's memory, significantly picked up or reflected "from her, on them which have understood" (72), in an image that intimately connects speaker and subject in a way that never materially occurred. Here the apprehension of good allows or gives birth to a new kind of life that is potentially stronger than that which went before (that is, the world with Drury in it) because of the knowledge of the loss. In this sense the idea of the death of Drury is linked back to the Fall itself. While the Fall is the worse thing that could have happened to a Christian, for a Christian humanist it also makes possible the best that could ever happen. Drury's death makes possible a new existence with the aid of those of understanding, like the poem's narrator, who act as midwife to the world's reconstruction. The youthful intactness of the virgin Drury makes possible a rejuvenated world as a fresh alternative to the decay and deterioration of the old world, graphically described in another birth image, as like the "sonnes of women after fifty" (204).

Elsewhere in the poems, the feminine is generally stereotypically negative—for example, in the images of Woman as the vehicle of man's ruin. Initially given by God for men's relief, made for "good ends" (103), Woman became and remains "accessory, and principall in ill" (104). From Adam and Eve resulted a situation in which all men now suffer at the hands of all women in a formulation where the poet positions his readers as male like himself.

> For that first marriage was our funerall:
> One woman at one blow, then kill'd us all,
> And singly, one by one, they kill us now.
> We doe delightfully our selves allow
> To that consumption; and profusely blinde,
> We kill our selves, to propagate our kinde.
>
> (105–10)

If the first "our" and "us" in these lines could possibly refer to all human beings as a result of the Fall ("our funerall," "us all"), then logically the second "us" cannot, but refers to a collective male "us" individually under attack in individual situations by individual women ("And singly, one by one, they kill us now"). Here the "us" and the following "We" at the beginning of the next line presuppose a male reader who will identify with the speaker in the shared predicament of their plight and the vulnerability of their sexual desire—undertaken, it seems, for the propagation of the race. In this construction, the speaker both acknowledges pleasure and constructs men as the willing victim or sacrifice through whom the continued existence of all human beings, including women, is guaranteed. Sexual reproduction is tainted by the curse of Eve and the male compulsion to engage in acts he knows to be tainted and tainting. The poet constructs here a male audience, sympathetic to his position, who with him look down upon the body of Woman, dissected and anatomized from their perspective and for their purposes.[12]

In a final image of "The First Anniversary" arising from the idea of the anatomy, and the interconnections between birth and death in so far as they relate to the occasion and purpose of the verse itself, the speaker directly articulates his own role. The paradox of the body's life being inversely related to the soul's appears in a familiar image of the body as the soul's prison. The earthly experience—which is all that the human being knows and to which it clings—is precisely that which holds the soul back from its own birth. Thus, Drury's death is actually the birth of her spirit or soul, argues the speaker in a step that marks the movement of the poem from lamentation of individual death and general mortality to the celebration of the possible and of what is to come. This is a movement in which the poet demonstrates the importance of his own role through positioning within the poem his own possible detractors. The speaker creates the possibility that there will be those who argue that Drury's qualities and the virtues that she comes to represent are not a fit topic for verse. Significantly, it is not that these people will criticize the fact of her being praised that readers are asked to consider but that it should be undertaken in verse. This hypothetical objection thus makes it possible, even necessary, for the speaker to undertake a defence of poetry and implicitly of himself. So it is that a poem that is occasioned by the death of a young stranger, and nominally concerns the state of the world, ends up by being an affirmation of the rights and responsibilities of the poet. Invoking the instruction of Moses by God to teach the people and "keep the song still in their memory" (466), the speaker thus positions himself as prophet and recorder. Significantly, the repetition of the personal pronoun "me" at the beginning of two lines near the end of the poem reinstates the importance of the speaker in relation to the subject of the poem who appears literally and metaphorically enveloped or overtaken by the poetic enterprise:

> Such an opinion (in due measure) made
> Me this great Office boldly to invade.

Nor could incomprehensiblenesse deterre
Me, from thus trying to emprison her.

(467–70)

The speaker thus makes a double revelation of himself, as poet and as user of the idea of the anatomy as a short term device. Logically, after all, an anatomy cannot continue indefinitely. There are only so many incisions that may be made before there is nothing left to incise: "But as in cutting up a man that's dead, / The body will not last out to have read / On every part" (435–37). If in some ways the body of the dead girl disintegrates before our very eyes throughout the poem, it is true to say that she was never there at all in any personal sense. And yet the poem has also become the only means by which she is embodied, imprisoned beyond the grave as a testament to the poet's skills, forever trapped in lines studied primarily because of Donne's renown for other verse. The ironies and contradictions extend outwards and ripple back over the circumstances of the poem's original moment of production, Donne's status in relation to Robert Drury and the poem as "business venture."[13] By the end of "The First Anniversary," the speaker has negotiated for himself a position of authority and stands triumphant beside the slab where poetry sits in place of Drury's body.

The tensions evident in images of the anatomy and the human body in "The First Anniversary" reappear in a startlingly violent form at the beginning of the second, in spite of the fact that this is not an anatomy but a "Progresse of the Soule." The fact that a year has passed might, the speaker suggests, persuade one to think that life after Drury would continue forever, yet the kind of life that exists is only that of the energy left over from the Drury world, "by force of that force which before, it wonne" (8). The poem's first image, then, is that of a ship with sails unfurled carried on by the momentum of the wind, which has now dissipated. The second, however, is considerably more violent: the image of a decapitated man whose head and neck stream blood, whose eyes twinkle, whose hands grasp in the last endeavors of the already dead. The graphic image of violent death is particularly inappropriate as an image associated with the young Elizabeth Drury but returns immediately to the previous poem's themes of birth and death and the facilities of the poet to see through to the meaning of bizarre events. What might be mistaken for life can be seen by those who understand to be other than it appears.

Shortly after this image of death occurs the image of birth with which I began this essay, an image that encapsulates the tensions between male poet and female subject.

> my life shal be,
> To bee hereafter prais'd, for praysing thee,
> Immortal Mayd, who though thou wouldst refuse
> The name of Mother, be unto my Muse,
> A Father, since her chast Ambition is,
> Yearely to bring forth such a child as this.
> These Hymes may worke on future wits, and so
> May great Grand-children of thy praises grow.
>
> (31–38)

Ironically, the reception of this poem represents a complete reversal of the path projected by the speaker. Far from the poem resulting in an increased admiration for her, Elizabeth Drury has become a problem that has to be explained before the poem can make sense and be understood. She is the woman problem at the heart of the poems that has to be interpreted. Far from being the source of the speaker/poet's fame, Elizabeth Drury and the *Anniversaries* are generally studied because they belong to Donne and to his canon, and therefore have to be accounted for. While they have been studied on their own, they are much less familiar to most readers than many of Donne's other poems. Far from Donne's fame relying on them, the *Anniversaries* have been seen as controversial intimations of a less sure and sophisticated writing skill.

That the denigration of himself before the subject of his verse is a commonplace, a poetic trope, is also suggested by the deliberate wittiness of the following images. Here, as in "A Funerall Elegie," which accompanied "An Anatomy" ("To scape th'infirmities which waite upone / Woman, shee went away, before sh'was one," 78), Drury is again positioned as female but not woman because of her early death. She escapes the slings and arrows hurled at the female of the species by dying before she could be caught up in sexuality and reproduction. Doubly fortunate Drury: dying while Donne was around to commemorate the death, and dying before being implicated by the physical and spiritual manifestations of her sexuality.

Described as a refusal of such implications, Drury's death is then made to seem an active moment of rejection, a denial of the most likely outcome of her continued existence in the world. After death, Drury's implication in the reproductive process is sanitized and undergoes a transformation whereby she takes on the male role of inseminator rather than that of the inseminated. The birth image here sees Drury and poet united in the reproductive act via the mediation of the poet's muse, whom Drury is to inspire so that the poet can give birth to the verses that will continue Drury's name. It is an asexual reproduction, without bodies, that creates the poet. The sexual roles are thereby reversed so that male poet takes on the female role that Drury left vacant. The conceit that arises from an exploration of Drury's gender and the sense of a womanly path left untrod produces a curious, deliberately witty, image that sees a temporary, ambiguous, feminization of the poet. The poet produces the verse, the yearly production of the child that is the commemoration of Drury's death, the anniversary poem, and thus is positioned as female in relation to the imagery of reproduction. That this is another kind of immaculate conception, however, is indicated by the tripartite nature of the conception (muse, Drury, poet), and the fact that only one of them has a concrete existence. Moreover, the reproduction is also a surrogate one since it is the muse, the abstracted essence of the poet, that actually gives birth rather than the poet himself. This second female "body" is also positioned as desireless in that her motivation is selfless and a "chaste Ambition" (35). While it is the muse rather than the poet who is ultimately positioned as the pregnant bearer of Drury's memory, residual impressions of a feminized poet contribute to a sense of the poem's awkwardness.

Tensions exist throughout the poem between a celebration of the young Drury as female and a general denigration of Woman. Drury can partly be celebrated precisely for escaping womanhood, for representing a chaste denial of femininity and for so doing becomes masculinized as the final reward. The insistence on Drury's chastity relies on invoking abstract ideas of virginity that may or may not have held any relationship to Drury's own life. It is important to reflect, too, that at fifteen Drury may have been considerably more sexualized than the poet encourages us to consider, a point that popular speculation about her death reinforces. Furthermore, given that what we see in the poems is more an idea of Drury as Woman than a negotiation of a woman's life presented by the poet, the birth of the poems and the poet also constitute an act of parthenogenesis in which the poet gives birth to himself in a perfect cycle of self-generation.

Yet if the poems themselves can be said to yield a picture of the poet as successful, if ambiguous, artificer, then the circumstances of its production and its physical manifestation in published form are rather more equivocal. The fact that there is a second anniversary has been said to testify to the success of the first and the demonstration of Donne's talents to the dead girl's parents. While the precise circumstances of the production of the poems are still not known, and critics argue over the relationship between "The Funerall Elegie" and "The Anatomy,"[14] it seems likely that the approval of the Drurys prompted the appearance of "The Second Anniversary." That the writing of a second poem had not been to the forefront of Donne's mind originally is indicated by the changes in the titles of the poem from 1611 when it was first published, to 1612 when it was published with the second poem. As the title pages of the published texts make clear, "An Anatomy" was designed to stand alone, whereas in the following year the two poems stand as companion pieces with subtitles (*The First Anniversarie: An Anatomie of the World; The Second Anniversarie; Of the Progress of the Soule*).[15] The poems collectively now known as the *Anniversaries* then appear to be a project that evolved rather than was planned from the beginning, dependent at least in part on patronage by the Drurys. The connections between Donne and the Drurys have been documented by various critics, notably Bald,[16] but the anxiety over the exact nature of the connection and its implications for Donne's poetry are reminiscent of concerns in Donne's own time. While acknowledging, for example, that the poems obviously demonstrated the existence of a relationship between Donne and the Drurys, Manley positions the poems as simply bringing the poet and patron together, skirting the possibility of patron commissioning poem. The relationship envisaged here is one of *nature* not finance.

> Donne was naturally drawn closer to the Drurys as a result of the *Anniversaries*, but he was never a servile dependent flattering the memory of his patron's daughter to secure a roof over his head. . . .[17]

Manley here reflects Donne's own regret, in a passage he quotes, at the publication of the poems, perhaps particularly in light of the less than favorable criticism they received. Having "descended" (as Donne saw it) to the level of publication his experience here presumably made him reluctant to publish his other works.[18] If writing for money was generally "considered ungentlemanly" in the seventeenth century,[19] then the possible taint of this accusation seems to provide at least one reason why Donne did not rush into print more often.

The title pages of the *Anniversaries* published in Donne's lifetime also indicate another interesting factor in the discussion of gender and power in the *Anniversaries*. Whilst Elizabeth Drury's name is not mentioned in the poems themselves, it is her name that stands on the title pages, not Donne's. While the printers' and sellers' names are included at the bottom of each separate title page, nowhere is Donne acknowledged as the author or producer of the poems. It seems there was no doubt that the poems were Donne's, but rather that his ownership of them was not an issue, perhaps for a couple of reasons. Firstly, of course, the whole notion of authorship was at a far more rudimentary level than it was later to become. Issues of copyright and its corollary censorship created the notion of the author as a legal and financially significant entity a little later on. Secondly, however, the absence of the author's name from the title page militates against accusations of personal aggrandizement and profit. When Parsons argues about the ungentlemanly nature of writing for profit, citing those people now known as writers who did not then so primarily identify themselves, Donne's name appears in the list.[20]

The title pages could be seen as demonstrating an inverse relationship to the poems regarding the relative significance of subject (and patron) and poet. The occasion and purpose of the poem are clearly stated at the gateway to the poems but become overshadowed by the atmosphere of poetry that dominates the poems themselves. Drury's name appears at the beginning of the poems, while she is absent from the poems as a whole. Conversely, it could also be that their provenance was well enough known to its prospective audience not to need advertising, unlike the name of the poems' nominal subject.

Throughout the verse known as the *Anniversaries*, the poet has been at pains to introduce and manipulate a wide range of metaphors and comparisons with which to reflect upon the dead girl as a means to reflection upon life itself. While Louis L. Martz saw the verse in terms of a series of spiritual exercises, it is also possible to see it as a series of exercises in writing. How flexible can the poet be within the framework of the elegy and anniversary? Here it is possible to underestimate the humor, as well as the wit, in the poems. A consciousness of hyperbole emerges at moments in lines where the poet seems to encourage readers to laugh at the excesses to which they have been brought. In the middle of "An Anatomy," for example, in a passage focused on the deterioration of the world, we find ourselves asked to believe that the disorder and disproportion in the world is such that the hills have grown and the seas deepened. The graphic and specific nature of the imagery combined with the regularity of the rhyme encourage a wry smile at the position to which hyperbole has led.

> Doth not a Tenarif, or higher Hill
> Rise so high like a Rocke, that one might thinke
> The floating Moone would shipwracke there, and sink?
> Seas are so deepe, that Whales being strooke to day,
> Perchance to morrow, scarse at middle way
> Of their wish'd journeys end, the bottom, dye.
>
> (286–291)

The self-consciousness characteristic of Donne's poetry generally is also evident in the *Anniversaries* in image after image that explores poetic making. This consideration of the relationship between poet and subject matter is nicely encapsulated in some lines toward the end of "The Second Anniversary," where the issue of writing itself is brought to the fore:

> shee rather was two soules,
> Or like to full, on both sides written Rols,
> Where eies might read upon the outward skin,
> As strong Records for God, as mindes within.
>
> (503–6)

This image sees Drury as roll, as written text, where the image of paper or parchment written on both sides is translated into an account of her interior and exterior perfection. The image can also be read, however, as an account of the poet's own practice in the preceding lines of the poem. The *Anniversaries* take Elizabeth Drury, the elegy, and the anniversary as material for the exercise of poetry and for exploring the idea of John Donne, poet.[21]

NOTES

1. C. H. Herford and Percy Simpson, *Ben Jonson: The Man and His Work* (Oxford: Clarendon Press, 1965), 1:133.
2. Herford and Simpson, *Ben Jonson*, 154.

3. Ruth A. Fox, "Donne's *Anniversaries* and the Art of Living," *ELH* 38 (1971): 528.

4. I am following Milgate's argument that "To the Praise of the Dead, and the Anatomy" and "The Harbinger to the Progress" are both by Joseph Hall; W. Milgate, *John Donne: The* Epithalamions, Anniversaries, *and* Epicedes (Oxford: Clarendon Press, 1978), 30.

5. "To the Praise of the Dead, and the Anatomy," 12–15. All references to the poems are to C. A. Patrides's ed. *The Complete English Poems of John Donne* (London: Dent, 1985).

6. C. S. Lewis, "Donne and Love Poetry in the Seventeenth Century," *Seventeenth Century Studies Presented to Sir Herbert Grierson* (Oxford: Clarendon Press, 1938), 79.

7. Herford and Simpson, *Ben Jonson*, 154.

8. From the third eclogues of Sidney's *Arcadia* (Harmondsworth: Penguin, 1977), also in *The Poems of Sir Philip Sidney*, ed. William A. Ringler Jnr. (Oxford: Clarendon Press, 1962), 85–90.

9. For example, we do not know the cause of Drury's death. Manley cites John Cullum's account of the varied local speculations: "According to one she was killed by her own father; according to another she was to have married the 'incomparable' Prince Henry, who also died an untimely death; and according to still another she loved a groom and died of grief when her father had him murdered," Frank Manley, *John Donne: The Anniversaries* (Baltimore: Johns Hopkins University Press, 1968), 1.

10. See, for example, Fox's distinctions between the two poems.

11. Jonathan Sawday, *The Body Emblazoned: Dissection and the Human Body in Renaissance Culture* (London: Routledge, 1995), 2.

12. A. D. Cousins, "Towards a Re-Consideration of Shakespeare's Adonis: Rhetoric, Narcissus, and the Male Gaze," *Studia Neophilologica* 68 (1996), also describes the way that Donne's persona, in other poems, "holds his version" of a woman "on display for the appreciative male gaze of the implied reader" (202).

13. Manley's phrase, in *John Donne*, 5.

14. See, for example, the different accounts given by Herbert J. C. Grierson, *The Poems of John Donne* (Oxford: Clarendon Press, 1912), 2:178; Manley, *John Donne*, 4–5; and Milgate, *John Donne*, xxix–xxx.

15. Grierson's edition helpfully includes copies of the title pages of the 1611, 1612, 1621 and 1625 editions.

16. R. C. Bald, *Donne and the Drurys* (Cambridge: Cambridge University Press, 1959).

17. Manley, *John Donne*, 5.

18. Donne cited in Manley, *John Donne*, 5.

19. Ian Parsons,"Copyright and Society," *Essays in the History of Publishing in Celebration of the 250th Anniversary of the House of Longmans 1724–1974*, ed. Asa Briggs (London: Longman, 1974), 35.

20. Parsons, "Copyright and Society," 35.

21. Kevin Pask refers to the distinction made between John Donne the poet, and Dr. John Donne the sermon writer: *The Emergence of the English Author: Scripting the Life of the Poet in Early Modern England* (Cambridge: Cambridge University Press, 1996), 115.

Donne the Snake Handler

Eugene D. Hill

Distinctive to the sermon as a literary form is its public unfolding in the real time of delivery. The preacher was frequently associated with the hourglass, whose snaking rope of sand governed the standard cycle of the hour in which the sermon was expected to run its course.[1] Donne often employs the image of the hourglass in his sermons—both reminding his auditors of the brevity of human life and no doubt assuring them of the preacher's awareness that he needs to draw to an end.[2] So sharp was John Donne's sense of the intricate curvature that the sermon represented as a form that he could play wittily on this shape in a late sermon whose topicality qua shapelessness has hitherto gone unrecognized.

In a recent essay, Jeanne Shami has delivered a salutary warning against "critics who profoundly mistrust the literal in poetry and appreciate the witty complexity of Donne's poetic strategies," yet "find nothing anomalous in reading the sermons literally, believing that Donne's beliefs are here straightforwardly addressed."[3] Shami comments on a number of (mainly Jacobean) sermons, demonstrating how "casuistically" hedged and double-edged is Donne's supposed adherence to absolutist claims—this even in the sermon of 1622 ostensibly defending James's restrictive *Directions to Preachers*. In the present study, I shall expand upon her work in two ways: first, by moving into the Caroline period; second, by attending not merely to complexities of argument (what Shami calls casuistry) but to the *formal* elements of a sermon that repay investigating with tools developed on Donne's poems: structure, voice, and (perhaps most importantly) emblem. The tools of the literary critic will prove necessary but not sufficient to this enterprise. If we are to understand Donne's wit, our readings must be informed by a sense of the ongoing life in London in the days that Donne mounted his pulpit and recited his emblematic Scriptural text.

What I mean by voice and emblem will emerge from a brief glance at a poem: no less an anthology piece than "The Funerall." The central object of the speaker's concern here—"The mystery, the signe" (line 4)—is the bracelet of hair, "the subtle wreath" that "crowns [his] arme" as his body is to be shrouded for burial (3).[4] Beginning in a tone of breathless worship, the poem moves inexorably and insidiously to its bitter final assertion. The beloved lady having rejected the speaker's advances, he now (whenever we take the moment of his final martyrdom to be) will exact his revenge: " 'tis some bravery, / That since you would have none of mee, I bury some of you" (23–25). The poem has shifted its addressee from the would-be shrouders of the opening lines ("Who ever comes to shroud me, do not harme / Nor question much . . . ," 1–2) to the specific lady, who knows all too well who she is. All too well because (the poem implies) if she doesn't allay the speaker's sensual agony before it's too late, he will incorporate his sole token of her into an emblem sufficiently powerful to mock her down through the centuries: the obscene image of possession, the bone penetrating the hairy circle. The reverently hushed opening has set us (readers, lady) up for a fall, a fall that takes place in and through our transformed understanding of the emblematic hair bracelet. The impudence of the stroke bears the indubitable signature of John Donne, the man whose very name (read it in Italian: *donne*) bespeaks his status as preeminent ladies' man.

To decipher the poet's formal signature on a sermon text, I will begin by bearing in mind the availability of what Christopher Hill (in his recent book, *The English Bible and the Seventeenth-Century Revolution*) calls "Biblical shorthand and codes." Avoiding the penalties prescribed for direct treatment in the pulpit of contemporary politics, preachers handled such matters by way of metaphor: "They could rely upon their readers' knowledge of the Scriptures." Indeed, Hill writes, in the period prior to 1640 "it could be a test of the preacher's ingenuity to see how far he could go with the aid of allusions and hints, without overstepping the limits." The printed text will not specify "the emphases, the gestures, the sidelong glances, by which a good preacher could convey much to his congregation."[5] So adept a scriptwriter as John Donne will have left some clues to direct us toward his dramatic subtext.

On January 25, 1628 (1629 N.S.; all subsequent dates hereafter given N.S.) Donne preached in the evening at St. Paul's on Acts 28.6. That day marks the Festival of the Conversion of St. Paul—an important day for Donne, and not merely because country lore held that it determined the weather for the entire year.[6] As Donne would explain at St. Paul's in 1630,

> The Book is called The Acts of the Apostles; But . . . it might be called the Acts of S. *Paul*, so much more is it conversant about him, then all the rest. In which respect, at this time of the yeare, and in these dayes, when the Church commemorates the Conversion of S. *Paul*, I have, for divers yeares successively, in this place, determined my selfe upon this Book. (Donne, *Sermons* 9:156)[7]

The significance of the Feast of Paul's Conversion for Donne can readily be accounted for. Since 1621 Donne had served as Dean of St. Paul's, London's main cathedral that bears the name of the city's patron saint. The English church, like every European church, saw itself as quintessentially *apostolic*, and Paul was the very model of the apostle, as Donne once explained: "whereas Christs other Disciples and Apostles, had a breeding under him, and came . . . first to be Disciples, and after to be Apostles; S. *Paul* was borne a man, an Apostle, not carved out, as the rest in time; but a fusil Apostle, an Apostle powred out, and cast in a Mold; As *Adam* was a perfect man in an instant, so was S. *Paul* an Apostle, as soone as Christ tooke him in hand" (6:207).

The first of Donne's four surviving sermons for this Festival handled a text from the very moment of conversion: "Saul, Saul, why persecutest thou me?" Auditors familiar with Donne's early years as a defiant Catholic whose personal motto was *"Antes muerto que mudado"*—meaning, as Dennis Flynn explains, "Rather dead than changed"—would catch the pertinence to the incumbent Dean.[9] A further connection will come clear if we recall the notorious state of the cathedral in this period: "an eyesore . . . the building decayed"; "the cathedral and Paul's Walk had become, rather than a shrine of worship, an exchange where daily gathered a concourse of merchants, money-changers, newsmongers . . . conversationalists, idle loiterers, worse still pickpockets and whores who hung around its doors and meandered through the Church itself. One poor old gentleman up from the country was arraigned for having defecated in St Paul's excused himself on the ground that he had not realized that he was in a church! His story was not incredible," adds Kevin Sharpe.[9] This was just the sort of place in which bold Paul had addressed the assembled curious townfolk—riffraff, merchants, shopkeepers, noblemen, informers—in one Mediterranean city after another in the Book of Acts. In 1630 Donne would write, "The Book is noted to have above twenty Sermons of the Apostles; and yet the Book is not called The Sermons, The Preaching of the Apostles, but the Practise, The Acts of the Apostles" (9:155–56). Precisely how richly emblematic such an enactment can be will become clear if we turn to the preacher's text for January 25, 1629.

Donne began: "ACTS 28.6. THEY CHANGED THEIR MINDS, AND SAID, THAT HE WAS A GOD" (8:312). The story comes from the final chapter of the Book of Acts, a book whose particular relevance for the divided church of the Renaissance Europe was widely acknowledged.[10] Paul and other prisoners are being transported to Rome for judgment by Caesar on charges of religious innovation; but they are shipwrecked on the island of Malta. Luke writes:

> And the barbarous people shewed us no little kindness: for they kindled a fire, and received us every one . . . And when Paul had gathered a bundle of sticks, and laid them on the fire, there came a viper out of the heat, and fastened on his hand. And when the barbarians saw the venomous beast hang on his hand, they said among themselves, No doubt this man is a murderer, whom, though he hath escaped the sea, yet vengeance suffereth not to live. And he shook off the beast into the fire, and felt no harm. Howbeit they looked when he should have swollen, or fallen down dead suddenly: but after they had looked a great while, and saw no harm come to him, they changed their minds, and said he was a god. (Acts 28.1–6; KJV)

As Calvin explains the story in a commentary in 1585 (translated into English), Paul "sealeth the former miracles [Oracula] with a new miracle; and so he ratifieth his apostleship among the men of Melita."[11] The chapter goes on to bring Paul to Rome, where he debates the Jews; the Book of Acts concludes abruptly with Paul preaching in Rome, under what is in effect house arrest (Acts 28.30–31).

The Maltese episode has not provoked a great range of homiletic response. Calvin offers the usual main points: the Maltese were deceived about Paul's spiritual condition, as "those men are deceived, who make this a general rule to judge every man according to his prosperity or adversity." Paul's "shaking off of the viper is a token of a quiet mind." Observing Paul's miraculous immunity, the Maltese jumped to the opposite extreme:

> This so wonderful and sudden a change ought to have inwardly touched the men of Melita, and to have moved them to give the glory to the mercy

of God, as they did before to vengeance. But as man's reason is always carried amiss unto extremities, they make Paul at a sudden a god, whom they took before to be a wicked murderer. But if he could not choose but be the one, it had been better for him to be counted a murderer than a god. And surely Paul would rather have wished to be condemned not only of one crime, but also to have sustained all shame, and to have been thrust down into the deep pit of hell, than to take to himself the glory of God. . . .

Calvin concludes that the Maltese "history doth witness that this is the fountain of superstitions, because men are unthankful to God, and do give his glory to some other." "Yea," Calvin explains, "this wickedness is in a manner born with us, to be desirous to adorn creatures with that which we take from God" (2:410–13).

Twentieth-century historical scholarship has devoted itself to compiling parallels to Paul's snake story in ancient literature Christian and pagan, historical and romantic; and to investigating ancient ideas about shipwreck and pollution.[12] This approach will help us little in understanding what Donne found in the Maltese story. We would do better to track an association within English literature: the Maltese mistaken apotheosis calls to mind the similar island-bound action of Caliban in Shakespeare's *Tempest*, who participates in a drunken communion as part of the foundation of a political commonwealth in which Stephano will be at once king and deity. *The Tempest* looks forever backward to Prospero's lost position as "absolute Milan" and forever forward to his return to rulership in Italy—much as Paul in this chapter of Acts is interrupted in a soon-to-be-resumed journey to the metropolis of Rome, where he must be judged by Caesar. Both texts direct our attention to royal judgment and royal neglect. Would such a connection have been prominent for Donne's audience on the Feast of St. Paul's Conversion 1629?

An excellent brief statement of what was going on in London can be found in a letter from Sir Francis Nethersole to the queen of Bohemia dated January 24, 1629, that is, one day earlier. As secretary to the Electress Palatine, Nethersole in a protracted correspondence kept this daughter of James I informed of doings in her younger brother's kingdom. Here is the précis of his report as it appears in the Calendar of State Papers:

The Parliament began again on Tuesday last. The King came not to the House as is usual. The next day, in the Commons they began to complain that the Petition of Right had been invaded in all the parts thereof. They were going further next day, and got heat in going, when Sec. Coke wished them to forbear till this day, when both Houses attending the King, he had declared, as for tonnage and poundage he had no thought of taking it by prerogative, or otherwise than as the gift of the people. This speech has given great satisfaction. The House of Commons is also much discontented with the printing of the Petition of Right with the several answers given thereto, and his Majesty's speech the last day of the Session, it having been first printed with the answer—*Droit soit fait comme il est désiré*,— and that impression afterwards suppressed. But that which troubleth them most is the recording that last speech of his Majesty in the Clerk's Book of the Commons' House since the recess. In matter of religion they are quiet as yet, but the greatest business is like to be about that. Mountague's book is called in by proclamation; the King has also pardoned Mountague, Cosin, Mainwaring, and Sibthorpe, but that will hardly save some of them. Lady Montgomery has fallen sick of the smallpox, whereupon the Queen has removed in haste to Somerset House.[13]

That last sentence aside, everything here has to do with the new session of Parliament, the ill-fated Parliament that opened on January 20. Ten days before its convening, the Venetian ambassador Contarini had reported that "good results are expected, as his Majesty is carefully preparing everything and will proceed more advisedly than he did before." A few days later the ambassador remains hopeful: "the king hopes for the best from parliament, and is holding it with the idea of coming to terms. Long consultations are held daily to this end. They intend to act firmly without vacillation, and not as they have done hitherto." But Contarini foresees vast consequences if king and Parliament fail in their efforts: of the "impending meeting of parliament," he writes: "If it does not agree with the king, England may be considered as no longer existing in the world, for she will be impotent for good or harm, and will have to attend to domestic affairs, and the means for raising money, of which there is so great a scarcity."[14]

Nethersole's letter shows what did happen in the first few days of the much anticipated session: all the old issues of money, of authority, and of religion reemerged in a virulent form. The Parliament of 1628 had been prorogued, leaving these matters unresolved. And the killing of Buckingham had left Charles free to be his own man at last, for better or worse; "With the death of Buckingham in August 1628 there is a very real sense in which the *personal* rule of Charles I may be said to have begun. Certainly contemporaries saw it so."[15] At first expectations had been high, but soon the old worries returned. Even Kevin Sharpe, as thoroughgoing (and as learned) an apologist for Charles as we are likely to have, reports that "a sense of weakness and decline, the consequence of military failure and domestic tension, pervades the political literature of 1628 and 1629."[16]

Every specification (smallpox aside) in Nethersole's letter tells a single story: that of Charles's combat with Parliament over the right to raise funds and maintain the vast authority to which he laid claim. This is not the place to work through each of the points; for my purposes, the most telling is that involving the last political figures mentioned, Mainwaring and Sibthorpe, whose names make frequent appearance in the state documents of 1628–29. Once we know who they are and what they stand for, we will be ready to reenter St. Paul's and watch Dr. Donne shape his talk.

Sibthorpe and Mainwaring were politically connected clerics who made reputations, and scandalized Parliament, by sermons delivered in 1627 in support of Charles's enforced loan.[17] Sibthorpe's sermon on February 22 (his text was Romans 13.7: "Render therefore to all their Dues") was presented to King Charles, who helped revise the piece and forced it into print by royal command when Archbishop Abbot refused to act on it. Sibthorpe insisted that he spoke not "as a *Syco-phanticall* Timeserver, nor as a *Statizing* Court Oratour; or one who had *left God to preach for the King;* as some are too apt uncharitably to censure; *unchristianly* dividing *God* and the King" (20).[18] As his due Sibthorpe received a post as chaplain-in-ordinary to the king; *DNB* also notes that "to prevent any danger to him from his sermon, he was included (24 Jan. 1629) in the pardon granted to Manwaring."

A more senior figure, already chaplain-in-ordinary to Charles since about 1626, Manwaring went much further than the unctuous Sibthorpe to avoid "dividing *God* and the *King.*" In July 1627 Manwaring preached a pair of sermons on Ecclesiastes 8.2: "I counsell thee, *to keepe the Kings commandement, and that in regard of the oath of God.*" His insistence that consent of parliament was not required for royal aids and subsidies enraged members of Commons,

> and on 9 June 1628 Pym carried up to the lords the charges which had been gradually collected against the preacher. He was charged with trying 'to infuse into the conscience of his majesty the persuasion of a power not bounding itself with law,' with seeking 'to blow up parliamentary powers, not much unlike Faux and his followers,' or, in the words of Pym, with 'endeavoring to destroy the king and kingdom by his divinity.' (*DNB*)

Manwaring was fined, suspended, and imprisoned in the Fleet. The book in which the two sermons had been published was suppressed. Manwaring's name, variously spelled, was a familiar one in the day. Nor was it quickly forgotten: in 1640 both the Short Parliament and the Long Parliament returned to this case, the latter imprisoning him and taking away all his preferments.

The remarkable feature of Roger Maynwaring's *Religion and Allegiance in Two Sermons Preached before the King's Maiestie* . . . [and published] *By His Maiesties Speciall Command* (1627) is the preacher's insistence that "this *high, large,* and most *constraining Power* of *Kings* . . . is not meerely *humane,* but *Superhumane,* and indeed no lesse then a *Power Divine.*" To make this point Manwaring repeatedly cites Psalms 82.6: "*I said yee are Gods.*" He spends several pages explaining in technical ways the unique "*participation* of Gods owne *Omnipotency*" that is enjoyed by Kings. He writes: "if we demand the *Reason,* why *Religion* doth thus associate *God,* and the *King,* It may be conceiued to be, from three *Causes* [each of which receives a paragraph of exposition]: Either from the Communion of Names . . . ; Or else, from the *Propinquitie,* and neere-bordering of such *Offences,* as reflect vpon *God,* and his anointed *King* . . . ; Or else, from that *Paritie* of *Beneficence,* which, Men enioy from *God,* and sacred *Kings.*"[19]

Manwaring's divinization of the earthly king has a long history behind it, going back at least to traditional misinterpretations of Aristotle's remark in Book 3 of *The Politics* that some men (traditionally read as kings) are so superior that it would be unjust to treat them in a state as equals: such a person would be "like a god among men" (1284a). Already in the 1580s, French constitutional theorists had reached the same position as Manwaring's. In his *Adversus Georgii Buchani dialogue, de iure regni apud Scotos, pro regibus apologia,* Adam "Blackwood carried the glorification of divinely authorized monarchy to its conclusion, stating that the person of the king, no less than his authority, was divine and that he was a god on earth in a literal sense."[20] In 1600 the Frenchified Scotsman William Barclay published his *De regno et regali potestate adversus Buchananum . . . et reliquos monarchomachos,* in which he quoted the legist Baldus to the effect that " 'The King of France is as the morning star shining in the midst of the southern mist, and therefore toward his own subjects he is as a certain corporal god, and is the animated law in his own realm. And thus what he does in the realm, not as he himself, that is, as a man, but as God, he does, whose Vicar he is in temporals.'"[21]

Barclay was widely read and frequently cited by political writers in the early seventeenth century. But one commentator on the divinity of kings Charles would indubitably have known: his father James I. In his *Speech to the Lords and Commons of the Parliament at White-Hall* (1610), James intoned:

> Kings are justly called gods for that they exercise a manner or resemblance of divine power upon earth. For if you will consider the attributes to God, you shall see how they agree in the person of a king. God has power to create, or destroy, make or unmake at his pleasure, to give life, or send death, to judge all, and to be judged nor accountable to none; to raise low things, and to make high things low at his pleasure, and to God are both soul and body due. And the like power have kings: they make and unmake their subjects; they have power of raising and of casting down, of life and death; judges over all their subjects, and in all cases, and yet accountable to none but God only. They have power to exalt low things and abase high things, and make of their subjects like men at the chess; a pawn to take a bishop or a knight, and to cry up or down any of their subjects, as they do their money . . .[22]

James had the good grace, of course, to temper his claim by a properly contextual citation of the relevant Psalm: "For in that same psalm where God says to kings *vos dii estis* [you are gods], he immediately thereafter concludes, 'But you shall die like men.' The higher we are placed, the greater shall our fall be." James draws the lesson: "Therefore all kings that are not tyrants, or perjured, will be glad to bound themselves within the limits of their laws" (107–9). James provides a standard reading for his day of the eighty-second Psalm: the text exalts kings ("Ye are gods"), but warns them to do justice, since "ye shall die like men, and fall like one of the princes" (verse 7). Twentieth-century Biblical scholarship reads the psalm as presenting "a trial in which God, as the head of the divine council, puts the pagan gods on trial."[23]

Without question, the Psalm text in which God was understood to call earthly kings gods was familiar to the seventeenth-century English, as we know not only from James but from Donne himself. On February 20, 1629, in a sermon at Whitehall, Donne will allude to 82.6 with a brevity that betokens familiarity:

> *Loquimini Deo*, speak to God; And *loquimini Diis*, speak to them whom God hath call'd Gods. As Religious Kings are bound to speak to God by way

of prayer; so those who have that sacred office, and those that have that Honorable office to do so, are bound to speak to Kings by way of Counsel. God hath made all good men *partakers of the Divine Nature*; They are *the sons of God*, The *seed of God*; But God hath made Kings partakers of his Office, and Administration. And as between man and himself, God hath put a Mediator, that consists of God and Man; so between Princes and People, God hath put Mediators too, who consider'd in themselves, retain the nature of the people (so Christ did of man) but consider'd in their places, have fair and venerable beams of his power, and influences of him upon them. And as our Mediator Christ Jesus found always his Fathers ears open to him; so do the Church and State enter blessedly and success-fully by these Mediators, into the ears of the King. (8:339–40)

The passage is striking for the way it links the Psalm verse with the celebrated problem of counsel. Donne was intensely aware of the di-lemma involved in offering unwelcome advice to a headstrong mon-arch; always before him must have been the example of his ancestor Thomas More. In a capital discovery published in 1970, John Gleason reported on Donne's marginal annotations (undated but probably around 1629) on a Latin text of More's *Utopia*. In the clearest terms Donne identified the abuses of the late 1620s with those of the previ-ous century satirized in the dialogue: "In the privacy of his study, the Dean likened these sycophants of More's day to the 'criers up of the Kings prerogative' in his own day"—the quoted phrase being one of the telling marginalia. Gleason believes that in his public role as preacher, Donne "himself became in the strongest terms a crier up of the King's prerogative." Indeed, Gleason goes so far as to suggest that one cause of the pronounced "melancholy" of Donne's last years was "his having to discharge his public duty in forms which were some-times opposed to his own convictions."[24]

But the sermon on the Feast of St. Paul's Conversion of 1629 tells a more complicated story, I believe. Given what his sophisticated audi-tors had on their minds on January 25, 1629, surely Donne's text would have evoked the Old Testament subtext of the Psalmist's *vos dii estis*. It is of course the nature of a subtext not to be stated. The preacher must maintain deniability. But he will employ voice, emblem and structure to make his point.

Donne once commented on the structural strength of "a winding staire:" "this is an act of the wisedome of the Serpent, which our Savi-our recommends unto us, in such a Serpentine line, (as the Artists call it) to get up to God, and get into God, by . . . degrees" (5:347). The snakelike lines prove particularly appropriate for what Donne called *"collaterall Increpation"* (5:200)—making an indirect but sharp reproof of the powerful. Such I take to be the emblematic form of the Dean's sermon of January 25, 1629: using the New Testament wisdom of serpents, Donne provokes in his congregation the thought of Charles's hypertrophied sense of the royal prerogative.

Donne plays the auditor like a fish on a line, giving a bit, withdrawing a bit. Take the opening words of Donne's sermon: "ACTS 28.6. THEY CHANGED THEIR MINDS, AND SAID, THAT HE WAS A GOD." Surely the audience would be primed for allusion to the Manwaring debate. But Donne implicitly corrects them: "The scene, where this canonization, this super-canonization (for it was not of a Saint, but of a God), was transacted, was the Ile of Malta: The person canonized, and proclaimed for a God, was S. *Paul*, at that time by shipwrack cast upon that Iland." So it's not Charles we're talking about, but Paul, though in the next few words Donne will interweave an allusion to Richard Mountague's book *Appello Caesarem*, which Nethersole accurately reported as having been suppressed (in fact on January 17): "S. *Paul* founde himself in danger of being oppressed in judgement, and thereby was put to a necesity of Appealing to *Caesar.* By vertue of that Appeale being sent to Rome, by Sea, he was surprized with such stormes, as threatned inevitable ruine." Donne blandly summarizes the story; but he also hints at the charges that the king was too close to the Catholic Church.

Donne's subtext comes closest to the surface, fittingly, at the center of his sermon, in the remarkable paragraphs 16–19 (pp. 322–25) of the thirty-five paragraph text. Donne begins paragraph 16 with a deadpan disclaimer: "But I move not out of mine own spheare; my spheare is your edification, upon this centre, The Proceeding of these men of *Malta* with S. *Paul*; upon them, and upon you I look directly, and I looke onely, without any glance, any reflection upon any other object." The language explicitly asks us to remain within the simple two-part division of the sermon: the Maltese first condemned Paul, then worshipped him; we, likewise, should avoid the extremes of overhasty condemnation and superstitious multiplication of divinities. But surely the words hint at what they deny, inviting our close scrutiny with a view to ascertaining another *object* of *reflection*.

Donne turns in paragraph 17 to "the incongruity of depending upon any thing in this world," concluding:

All the world never joyned to deceive one man, nor was ever any one man able to deceive all the world. *Contemptu famae contemnuntur & virtutes*, was so well said by *Tacitus*, as it is pity S. *Augustine* said it not, They that neglect the good opinion of others, neglect those vertues that should produce that good opinion. Therefore S. *Hierom* protests to abhor . . . that vulgar, that street, that dunghill language, *Satis mihi*, as long as mine owne conscience reproaches me of nothing, I care not what all the world sayes. We must care what the world sayes, and study that they may say well of us. But when they doe, though this be a faire stone in the wall, it is no foundation to build upon, for *They change their minds* (323).

After this giddy cadenza on vicissitude and conscience, Donne offers a paragraph (18) that bears the italicized marginal gloss *Populus*, then another (19) glossed *Principes*. If sermon time is determined by the snakelike figure of the hourglass, this is the constricted center, where meaning and expression are under tightest pressure.

In paragraph 18 Donne follows standard commentary in reproving the Maltese common people for fickleness of opinion. The Swiss Protestant Rudolph Gualther in his commentary of 1562 had done so as well, and then gone on to attack the Roman Catholic Church for its pagan-like readiness to multiply religious entities—a Satanic way, Gualterus observes, to contaminate the true faith. Donne will make the same point, somewhat more temperately, later on in critique of the Romanists.[25] But Gualther has nothing to say about the dangers of princely misjudgment, which Donne boldly introduces into the center of his sermon text.

Picking up the final words of paragraph 17 (*"They change their minds"*), number 18 begins:

Who do? our text does not tell us who: The story does not tell us of what quality and condition these men of Malta were, who are here said *to have changed their minds*. Likeliest they are to have beene of the vulgar, the ordinary, the inferiour sort of people, because they are likeliest to have flocked and gathered together upon this occasion of *Pauls* shipwrack upon that Iland. And that kinde of people are alwaies justly thought to be most subject to this levity, *To change their minds*.

So far, so conventional. But then Donne makes a surprising move:

The greatest Poet layes the greatest levity and change that can be laid, to this kinde of people; that is, *In contraria*, That they change from one

extreame to another; *Scinditur incertum studia in contraria vulgus.* Where
that Poet does not onely meane, that the people will be of divers opinions
from one another; for, for the most part they are not so; for the most part
they think, and wish, and love, and hate together; and they doe all by example, as others doe, and upon no other reason, but therefore, because
others doe. Neither was that Poet ever bound up by his words, that hee
should say *In contraria,* because a milder, or more modified word would
not stand in his verse; but hee said it, because it is really true, The people
will change into contrary opinions; And whereas an Angel it selfe cannot
passe from East to West, from extreame to extreame, without touching
upon the way betweene, the people will passe from extreame to extreame,
without any middle opinion; last minutes murderer, is this minutes God,
and in an instant, *Paul,* whom they sent to be judged in hell, is made a
judge in heven. The people wil change. *In the multitude of people is the Kings
honour* [margin: Prov. 14.28).

The Dean goes on to offer one example from Roman history and several examples from Biblical history of the difficulty of controlling the
people, then concludes his paragraph: "Therefore we must say with
the Prophet [margin: Ier. 17.5], *Cursed be the man, that trusteth in man,
and maketh flesh his arme, and whose heart departeth from the Lord.* For,
They, the people, *will change their minds.*"

In this complex passage, Donne insists that Virgil, as supreme poet,
must control his words with ultimate precision. So if the Roman writes
that the people move from one extreme to another, he must mean
precisely that. And Donne too moves in this paragraph: from the care-
ful fussy voice of a grammarian to the intense monitory tones of a
prophet, warning his king that excesses, such as self-deification, inevitably bring on their contraries. The dazzling jump in this passage from
the exegesis of Virgil to the monitory wisdom of the Old Testament
becomes even more powerful when we catch the allusion here to the
Aeneid, book 2, verse 39, which the Loeb translator renders: "The wa-
vering crowd is torn into opposing factions." Aeneas is telling Dido
the story of how Troy fell. At this moment the people are debating
whether or not to admit the Trojan horse that will be their undoing.
The next lines usher in Laocoon, who will warn the people before suc-
cumbing to the deadly embrace of the serpents. Old Troy's fall, as so
often in English literature, adumbrates a threat to Troynovant—that
is, to England.

Paragraph 19, with its marginal note *"Principes,"* begins as follows:

But yet there is nothing in our text, that binds us to fixe this levity upon the people onely. The text does not say, That there was none of the Princes of the People, no Commanders, no Magistrates present at this accident, and partners in this levity. Neither is it likely, but that in such a place as Malta, an Iland, some persons of quality and command resided about the coast, to receive and to give intelligence, and directions upon all emergent occasions of danger, and that some such were present at this accident, and gave their voyce both wayes, in the exclamation, and in the acclamation, That hee was *a murderer*, and that he was *a God*. For, *they will change thier minds*; All, High as well as low, will change.

Donne proceeds to cite "A good Statesman," Polybius, who

sayes, That the people are naturally as the Sea; naturally smooth, and calme, and still, and even; but then naturally apt to be moved by influences of Superiour bodes; and so the people apt to change by them who have a power over their affections, or a power over their wils. So, sayes he, the Sea is apt to be moved by stormes and tempests; and so, the people apt to change with rumors and windy reports. So, the Sea is moved, So the people are changed, sayes *Polybius*.

Reversing his argument here, Donne abandons the standard interpretation of his sermon text. The people are divided because of the failures of their *principes*; the latter bear the true blame for the sea-change. Donne insists on this point as he continues:

But Polybius might have carried his politique consideration higher then the Sea, to the Aire too; and applied it higher then to the people, to greater persons; for the Aire is shaked and transported with vapours and exhalations, as much as the sea with winds and stormes; and great men as much changed with ambitions in themselves, and flatteries from others, as inferiour people with influences, and impressions from them.

The paragraph ends with praise of the Lord, who cannot change, and a further warning: "for they, who depend upon their love, who can change, are in a wofull condition. And that involves all; all can, all will, all do change, high and low."

Donne's "politique consideration" here upstages that of the "good Statesman Polybius": not the people so much as the prince merits chiding for introducing disorder in the island. When, early in paragraph 20, Donne cites the Psalmists (118.9) to the effect that "*It is better to trust in the Lord, then to put confidence in Princes*," one cannot readily imagine that the Dean's auditors would have neglected to make the contemporary application. In condemning "this hasty acclamation of theirs, *He is a God*" (327), Donne is subtextually but powerfully mocking the recent claims for Stuart absolutism as given voice by Manwaring among others. For Donne, the Caroline pretensions represented an *innovation* ("they changed their minds"), therefore a danger for the island nation. Using the wisdom of serpents, the innocence of doves (Matt. 10.16)—a sharp subtext keyed to the week's events, a generalized literal surface that draws some nontopical moral lessons—Donne creates a sermon whose shape does real work. Donne catches his auditors' attention—and, perhaps, his monarch's conscience—on his serpentine line of *"collaterall Increpation."*

The sermon ends, as Donne's sermons often do, with an appeal to the Trinity, the final words being "the holy Ghost. *Amen.*" In this case, Donne might want us to remember that the power to handle snakes was one of the gifts of the Spirit (Mark 16.18)—a point often made in discussions of the Maltese story, for example by Gualther.[26] Some of Donne's friends might well have recalled the ancestral emblem of the Donne family: a sheaf of snakes (10:26). Here, as in the poem I cited earlier, Donne has inscribed his personal emblem on the text, shaped it in his image, leaving us (his auditors and readers) to admire the canniness of John Donne the Good Statesman. Dealing with the hot events of the moment, playing with fire—Donne operates with the aplomb of the snake handler. Not that he spoke, I would suggest, without a measure of trepidation; that would only heighten the performance. Calvin insisted that in dealing with the viper, Paul was bold, but not without fear (2:412). For Donne as well, we may readily believe, on the day of this sermon apprehension was overcome by confidence in the apostolically protected (and emblematically represented) exercise at hand.[27]

NOTES

1. John Sparrow, "John Donne and Contemporary Preachers," in *Essays and Studies by Members of the English Association*, vol. 16, ed. H. J. C. Grierson (Oxford: Clarendon, 1931), 157n.

2. Eiléan Ní Chuilleanáin, "Time, Place and the Congregation in Donne's Sermons," in *Literature and Learning in Medieval and Renaissance England: Essays Presented to Fitzroy Pyle,* ed. John Scattergood (Blackrock, Co. Dublin: Irish Academic Press, 1984), 211–13.

3. Jeanne Shami, "Donne's Sermons and the Absolutist Politics of Quotation," in *John Donne's Religious Imagination: Essays in Honor of John T. Shawcross*, ed. Raymond-Jean Frontain and Frances M. Malpezzi (Conway: University of Central Arkansas Press, 1995), 382.

4. Quotations from Donne's poems are from *The Complete English Poems of John Donne*, ed. C. A. Patrides (London: Dent, 1985).

5. Christopher Hill, *The English Bible and the Seventeenth-Century Revolution* (London: Allen Lane, 1993), 54–55, 78.

6. Dorothy Gladys Spicer, *Yearbook of English Festivals* (New York: Wilson, 1954), 27.

7. Quotations from Donne's sermons are from *The Sermons of John Donne*, ed. Evelyn M. Simpson and George R. Potter, 10 vols. (Berkeley: University of California Press, 1958). Passage quoted is from 9: 156.

8. Dennis Flynn, *John Donne and the Ancient Catholic Nobility* (Bloomington: Indiana University Press, 1995), 1–3.

9. Kevin Sharpe, *The Personal Rule of Charles I* (New Haven and London: Yale University Press, 1992), 322.

10. In 1524, dedicating his *Paraphrase on Acts* to the new Pope, Erasmus wrote: "I could not fail to compare the very turbulent and corrupt state of the church in our own day with the kind of church of which Luke has given us such a wonderful picture in this book"; Desiderius Erasmus, *Paraphrase on Acts*, ed. J. Bateman, trans. R. Sider, *Complete Works of Erasmus*, vol. 50 (Toronto: University of Toronto Press, 1995), 2.

11. John Calvin, *Commentary upon the Acts of the Apostles*, ed. Henry Beveridge, trans. Christopher Featherstone (Grand Rapids, MI: Eerdmans, 1957), 2:409. Hereafter, references are given in the text.

12. For a guide to the literature see Ernest Haenchen, *The Acts of the Apostles: A Commentary* (Philadelphia: Westminster, 1971), 712–14; and Luke Timothy Johnson, *The Acts of the Apostles* (Collegeville, MN: Liturgical Press, 1992), 461–67.

13. *State Papers, Domestic Series, . . . of the Reign of Charles I, 1628–1629*, vol. 3. John Bruce (London, 1859), 456.

14. *Calendar of State Papers and Manuscripts Relating to English Affairs Existing in the Archives and Collections of Venice*, vol. 21, ed. Allen B. Hinds (London: 1916; rpt. Neldeln/Lichtenstein: Kraus, 1970), 493, 503.

15. Sharpe, *The Personal Rule of Charles I*, 49.

16. Sharpe, *The Personal Rule of Charles I*, 61.

17. I follow DNB entries for both men.

18. Richard Sybthorpe, *Apostolike Obedience. Shewing the* Duty *of* Subjects *to pay* Tribute *and* Taxes to their *Princes*, according to the *Word* of God, in the *Law* and the *Gospell*. . . . London, 1627. Facsim. rpt. Amsterdam: Theatrum Orbis Terrarum, 1976, 20, In quoting from seventeenth-century books I silently remove the long s.

19. Roger Maynwaring, *Religion and Allegiance in Two Sermons* (London: 1627); passages cited are from pages 10–11 of the first sermon, and 22–24 of the second, which is separately paginated.

20. William Farr Church, *Constitutional Thought in Sixteenth-Century France* (Cambridge: Harvard University Press, 1941), 248.

21. William Barclay, *The Kingdom and the Regal Power by William Barclay, Paris, 1600*, trans. George Albert Moore (Chevy Chase, MD: Country Dollar Press, 1954), 360–61.

22. James I, "Speech to the Lords and Commons of Parliament at White-Hall," in

Divine Right and Democracy: An Anthology of Political Writing in Stuart England, ed. David Wootton (Harmondsworth: Penguin, 1986), 107–9.

23. William L. Holladay, *The Psalms through Three Thousand Years* (Minneapolis: Fortress, 1993), 22. For the main studies of the Psalm, see Marvin E. Tate, *Psalms 51–100. World Biblical Commentary*, vol. 20 (Dallas: Word, 1990).

24. John B. Gleason, "Dr. Donne in the Court of Kings: A Glimpse from Marginalia," *JEGP* 69 (1970): 603, 611.

25. Rodolphus Gualterus [Rudolph Gualther], *In acta apostolorum per divum lucam descripta, homiliae CLXXV* (Tiguri, 1562), 284, 329–30.

26. Gualterus, *In acta apostolorum*, 284.

27. I should mention one further possibility. The idea of linking Charles' absolutist claims may have come to Donne by way of another recent event. Reports would have reached the Dean of the experience in August of his friend Sir Thomas Roe, who was on board the ship *Sampson* when "She fought 26 hours with four galley of Malta about a sea compliment; the Maltese commanding her to strike her flag for the great masters of Malta, and the English bidding them strike for the King of England." See *Calendar of State Papers*, ed. Hinds, 280 including note.

WORKS CITED

Barclay, William. *The Kingdom and the Regal Power by William Barclay, Paris, 1600.* Translated by George Albert Moore. Chevy Chase, MD: Country Dollar Press, 1954.

Calendar of State Papers and Manuscripts Relating to English Affairs Exisiting in the Archives and Collections of Venice . Vol. 21. Edited by Allen B. Hinds. London, 1916. Repr. Neldeln/Lichtenstein: Kraus, 1970.

Calvin, John. *Commentary upon the Acts of the Apostles.* Edited by Henry Beveridge from the English translation of Christopher Fetherstone. 2 vols. Grand Rapids, MI: Eerdsmans, 1957.

Church, William Farr. *Constitutional Thought in Sixteenth-Century France.* Cambridge: Harvard University Press, 1941.

Donne, John. *Complete English Poems of John Donne.* Edited by C. A. Patrides. London: Dent, 1985.

———. *The Sermons of John Donne.* 10 vols. Edited by Evelyn M. Simpson and George R. Potter. Berkeley: University of California Press, 1958.

Erasmus, Desiderius. *Paraphrase on Acts.* Edited by J. Bateman. Translated by R. Sider. *Complete Works of Erasmus.* Vol. 50. Toronto: University of Toronto Press, 1995.

Flynn, Dennis. *John Donne and the Ancient Catholic Nobility.* Bloomington: Indiana University Press, 1995.

Gleason, John B. "Dr. Donne in the Court of Kings: A Glimpse from Marginalia." *JEGP* 69 (1970): 599–612.

Gualterus, Rodolphus. *In acta apostolorum per divum lucam descripta, homiliae CLXXV.* Tiguri, 1562.

Haenchen, Ernst. *The Acts of the Apostles: A Commentary.* Philadelphia: Westminster, 1971.

Hill, Christopher. *The English Bible and the Seventeenth-Century Revolution*. London: Allen Lane, 1993.

Holladay, William L. *The Psalms through Three Thousand Years*. Minneapolis: Fortress, 1993.

James I. *Speech to the Lords and Commons of the Parliament at White-Hall. Divine Right and Democracy: An Anthology of Political Writing in Stuart England*. Edited by David Wootton. Harmondsdworth: Penguin, 1986.

Johnson, Luke Timothy. *The Acts of the Apostles*. Collegeville, MN: Liturgical Press, 1992.

Maynwaring, Roger. *Religion and Allegiance in Two Sermons.* . . . London, 1627.

Ní Chuilleanáin, Eiléan. "Time, Place and the Congregation in Donne's Sermons." In *Literature and Learning in Medieval and Renaissance England: Essays Presented to Fitzroy Pyle*, edited by John Scattergood, 197–215. Blackrock, Co. Dublin: Irish Academic Press, 1984.

Shami, Jeanne. "Donne's Sermons and the Absolutist Politics of Quotation." In *John Donne's Religious Imagination: Essays in Honor of John T. Shawcross*, edited by Raymond-Jean Frontain and Frances M. Malpezzi, 340–412. Conway: University of Central Arkansas Press, 1995.

Sharpe, Kevin, *The Personal Rule of Charles I*. New Haven and London: Yale University Press, 1992.

Spicer. Dorothy Gladys. *Yearbook of English Festivals*. New York: Wilson, 1954.

State Papers, Domestic Series, . . . *of the Reign of Charles I, 1628–1629*. Vol. 3. Edited by John Bruce. London, 1859.

Sparrow, John. "John Donne and Contemporary Preachers." In *Essays and Studies by Members of the English Association*, vol. 16, edited by H. J. C. Grierson, 144–78. Oxford: Clarendon, 1931.

Sybthorpe, Richard. *Apostolike Obedience. Shewing the* Duty *of* Subjects *to pay* Tribute *and* Taxes to their *Princes*, according to the *Word* of *God*, in the *Law* and the *Gospell* . . . . London, 1627. Facsim. rpt. Amsterdam: Theatrum Orbis Terrarum, 1976.

Tate, Marvin E. *Psalms 51–100. Word Biblical Commentary*. Vol. 20. Dallas: Word, 1990.

Recent Genre Criticism of the Works of John Donne

Damian Grace

Faced with an almost scandalous range of incompatible conclu-sions afflicting modern interpretations of Donne's *Anniversaries*, Rosa-lie Colie concluded that Donne broke boundaries of style and theme and created "a new coherence" in which "the poems consciously ex-ploit playfully and seriously a great many literary genres available to the Renaissance poet."[1] If one problem of criticism is imposed coher-ence, another—according to Colie—is too restrained and formal a reading of texts that conflated forms and styles that we prefer to sepa-rate. In her acclaimed book *The Resources of Kind*, Colie set the tone for subsequent use of genre in critical interpretation of Renaissance texts. She rejected discussion in terms of "a rigid system of genres—which, really, never existed in practice and barely even in theory" in favor of "a body of almost unexpressed assumptions, many of them versions of classical theory or practice, which took for granted certain basic rules of expression."[2] It is not only genre that is disputed in Re-naissance literature but the question of genre and its implications for interpretation. Nowhere is this better illustrated than in criticism of the works of Donne.

Genre is not a cipher with which to decode Donne's works. In fact, very few authors address it directly as a means of appraisal. Mostly genre is subsumed as part of other critical discussions, not as uniquely offering a way to understanding. Even Barbara Estrin's recent work on gender and genre, *Laura*, is more concerned with the social and sexual resources that Donne could employ to endow the women in his work with a poetic sensibility and autonomy than with the possibilities of kind in Colie's sense: gender variations take center stage and genre is merely supporting.[3] Another example of implicit genre criticism is Richard Halpern's attempt to move beyond an impoverished Marxist criticism and an unreflective New Criticism in treating Donne's *Songs and Sonnets* as examples of autonomous poetry sustained by autopoeisis. Halpern's argument that sexuality became an autonomous sphere in life and poetry—the Renaissance love sonnet—only makes sense if one finds Marxist criticism compelling in the first place, but it nonetheless presents an implicit appeal to genre. The mistress in a Renaissance sonnet "tends to become a mere triggering device whose specific characteristics become increasingly irrelevant," for a matrix of conventions autopoietic in nature now sustain the poem apart from any social context in which it might be written. This is at once a strong sense of convention and a weak one: genre enables the autonomy of the love poem, but this genre is in consequence disconnected from the world and has become fantastic and self-referential. Halpern builds his case without reference to genre or convention as organizing principles, but they are immanent to it and sustain it.[4]

Genre, then, has been central to Donne controversies and the interpretations of some of his most perceptive critics, even if not always acknowledged as such. It was central to the symposium sponsored by the *John Donne Journal* on "Satyre III" in 1991, in which Camille Wells Slights, Paul Sellin, and Thomas Hester show how elastic genre criticism can be. This is the scandal for which Colie sought a rational explanation, but as she has argued, genre is not determinative either for author or critic. For both it provides resources of kind, and in the symposium this is cause for thanks rather than regret.

Camille Wells Slights argues that "Satyre III" should not be read as Donne's radically youthful rejection of Catholicism on his way to middle-aged Protestantism. She rejects the biographical interpretations sometimes imposed on this satire and gives it an interpretation oriented by genre instead. Why, she asks, would Donne have chosen a form so closely associated with social criticism in order to work out the personal challenge of religious conviction? Her answer is that Donne was less concerned in "Satyre III" with personal religious questions than with the problem of translating religious adherence into social participation.[5]

"Satyre III" is not a poem that debates doctrine, but one that attempts to rouse its implied young male reader from apathy to search for the true religion. The satire of religion points not only to manifest failures but also to the imperfection of the process of discernment. It is as easy to be wrong about religious choices as about other aspects of life.[6]

Donne insists not on doctrine but on the correct ways of searching for religious truth, that way being to "doubt wisely." In other words, "Satyre III" is not an injunction to doubt nor an expression of it. Wise doubt is an interlocutory process that, according to Slights, is not introspective. It involves asking questions of others, not oneself.

Genre dictates possibilities here. As an instrument for the examination of one's beliefs, satire will not do the job. Satire is better suited to the task of engagement, to wise participation in community—that is, engagement that recognizes authority without enjoining mere conformity and dismisses introspection in favor of "the dialectical process of participating in human debate."[7] In this reading, genre is the hinge on which the argument turns. Without the specifically social reference of the satirical form, "Satyre III" could be read as a purely personal struggle with religious conscience.

Paul Sellin takes issue with this kind of interpretation, finding in "Satyre III" a dramatic monologue with more of a family resemblance to "The Crosse" than to the satirical poems with which it is grouped. Sellin questions the place of "Satyre III" amongst Donne's satires, pointing out that it is separated from them not only by the subject matter of personal religious struggle but also by meter and form. For Sellin, there is enough uncertainty about the genre of "Satyre III" to make it questionably part of Donne's *liber satyrarum*.[8] This in turn must color interpretation. Now the religious element is more personally pressing and Slights's socially based wise doubt recedes in importance. The question on Sellin's terms seems to be, "Where is one to find true religion?" rather than the interlocutory question, "where is true religion to be found?"

The third member of the *JDJ* symposium, Thomas Hester, tackles head-on the issue raised by Sellin. Central to Hester's interpretation is the fact that "Of Religion" is "above all a *satire*."[9] Citing Shawcross, Hester points to the fact that "Satyre III" always appears in manuscript with at least two other satires and never alone. Directly answering the challenge of Sellin, Hester insists on a reading of "Satyre III" that resists assimilating it to "meditation, oration, . . . verse epistle, personal apologia, . . . or unequivocal revelation of precisely where Donne himself stood . . . in the Counter-Reformation wars of truth."[10] The object of the satire is Elizabethan England's "idolatry in which all 'masculine' force . . . must be exerted to glorify a political 'Mistresse' . . . who has appropriated only the appearances or 'names' of Christ's Bride."[11] Here Hester departs also from Slights. Satire for him is firmly anchored in social context, but it is also deeply personal:

it is a way for Donne to cling to the vestiges of his Catholicism in the face of the loss of free will and the political imposition of Protestantism.

While Sellin cleaves to a view of satire that effectively excludes "Satyre III" from Donne's satirical canon, Slights and Hester apply the insights of Colie to discover a broad range of concerns in the poem that would be excluded by an emphasis on strictly policed and pure genre.

Heather Dubrow[12] argues that far from trying to evade the difficulties that genre could present for a poet constrained to work under the patronage system, Donne positively embraced them: "he wrote epithalamia not in spite of but rather because of the many conventions with which the genre is laden. He appears . . . to have welcomed the challenge of playing the traditions of that genre against the demands of his individualistic talent."[13] Because of the well-established conventions of the wedding poem, Donne's variations on the form can be documented.

Dubrow makes her point in two separate interpretations of epithalamia, which may usefully be compared. In "An Epithalamium or Marriage Song on the Lady Elizabeth . . . ," Donne acclaims the wedding of Princess Elizabeth to the Elector Palatine, a prince that his erstwhile patron, Sir Robert Drury, had recently contrived to insult. If Donne hoped his poem would distinguish him from his patron, he would soon find himself compelled to write a second celebration of a wedding in even more ticklish circumstances. The second wedding poem, "An Epithalamium at the Marriage of the Earl of Somerset," was offered some time after the marriage of Robert Carr, Viscount Rochester and Lady Frances Howard. The patronage of the impolitic Drury having proved barren, circumstances compelled Donne to oblige a new patron, Rochester, with a celebratory lyric. As Donne had entered Rochester's employment after the death of his friend, Sir Thomas Overbury, for whose murder Frances Howard was tried, and had laced his suit to Rochester with unrestrained flattery, it is not surprising that the poet's muse had difficulty obliging. His scruples must surely have been tried. Some critics reject this out of hand, making Donne the hireling of Rochester in all his designs.[14] The problem for Donne—if he did scruple more than a little—was to conform to the demands of the occasion poetically, while retaining something of his dignity in celebrating an infamous alliance. The conventions of the lyric epithalamium had to be met without suggesting that the bride and groom had long been the subject of gossip, and that the lady's reputation for virtue had been defeated by the taint of adultery and murder. Donne's performance in the ensuing lyric has, in consequence, been criticized as lacking in integrity and wanting poetic skill.

Dubrow shows that such simple judgments miss the subtlety of Donne's modulations of the epithalamium lyric form to make politically pointed observations and outright censures from a position of safety. Praise, sometimes blatantly offered, and blame, often given through indirection, are commingled in this work. In the Elizabeth epithalamium, Donne opens with a sacralizing but undeferential reference to St. Valentine, whose day it is. No invocation of pagan gods here. Then he approaches the convention of praising bride and groom with restraint. The central concern of producing heirs is then subordinated to the sexual bond between the couple, and the politics of reproduction is diminished. The same fate awaits the depiction of the marriage ceremony, for religion too is diminished, as well as the social codes it mediates. In other words, Dubrow argues that the focus of the day is on the relationship of the couple and their happiness, not on the social function of the union. Dubrow draws a parallel between the message Donne sends the couple about observing social codes and the stance he adopts himself towards the literary codes governing the epithalamium.[15]

The praise of Rochester and Howard is, by contrast, easy and obvious as flattery. Oddly, however, James I is praised, hinting at his extensive role in ensuring that Rochester and Howard are joined. If the classic versions of the lyric form demand a reconciliation of conflicting dynastic and sexual tensions in marriage, Donne could not give this couple the approval to flout social codes that he had given Elizabeth and the Elector. Rochester and his bride had a past. Quite the reverse: the need for conciliation is so tempered that the poet actually urges the consummation that Rochester and Howard had already celebrated. The matter of heirs is glossed in deference to the barrenness of Frances Howard's marriage to the earl of Essex. But the role of the church in blessing the union is amplified here, in order to give the couple the semblance of religious motivation. In contrast with the earlier epithalamium, Dubrow argues that Donne's handling of generic conventions allows him to confer ostensible praise on the couple, while continually distancing his audience and the community from the proceedings. They do not need to be warned about social codes and the price of consilience: they have broken the former and brokered the latter. They are a spectacle, a theatrical performance that is only nominally public. Everybody observes but few participate. The secret of Rochester and Howard is open but cannot be stated. The distance of the author and his reader from the wedding removes them from complicity in it and evades the need for polite face making according to court policy.

Genre cuts two ways. Used in an expository way, it can reveal the conventions and the departures from them operating within a text. It can also be a way of appraising a work. If a poem is described as "conventional," then its worth is immediately depreciated. Likewise, attributions of 'uniqueness' imply a departure from conventions and a concomitant originality. Both extremes would, of course, be unintelligible. A unique poem, whatever else it might be, would no more be cut off from conventions of some kind than a merely conventional one would be wholly composed of them. Such attributions of worth and deficiency miss the point. Adherence to conventions can misleadingly suggest that genres are templates for writing rather than the products of writing. Genres grow out of bodies of work, not vice-versa. Genre is a language to be spoken, not a set of rules for composition. It is the instrument to be played, not the tune. The question that finally matters is not whether conventions are invoked (this question now being depleted of any discursive value), but how they are used. This, of course, is to take one side in the politics of literary criticism, namely the rhetorical. Thomas Sloane has contrasted the formalist and the rhetorical approaches to genre. For Sloane, the formalist approach implies a static deployment of convention in poetry and an indifference to audience; the rhetorical, by contrast, is always aware of its audience and treats conventions as strategies of communication whether in poetry or other forms.[16] In some ways, John Shawcross could be seen as belonging to the formalist school, but in stressing the internal coherence of convention in the making of a poem he does not forget biographical and social context; he simply relegates them to the background and places the poet's use of poetic and linguistic conventions in the foreground.[17]

Genres, as Colie has argued, are dynamic, not static. That they are compendia of resources does not mean that they are static, for they may be used well or ill, not only by authors but by their readers and critics. At their most powerful, they are not present to consciousness. For precisely that reason, however, the modern critic—Halpern provides a good instance of this—finds in them the way to gain access to shared assumptions and individual intentions through the reading of texts. Pressed too hard, genre criticism can go the way of Marxist theory, so that every text and the analysis of it offers the opportunity to recapitulate a particular ideology. Conceivably, every essay in Donne criticism could be squeezed into generic service. Renunciation of genre as the universal key to unlock the complexities of Donne's works should not imply that it has nothing to disclose. Nor should the variety of plausible disclosures scandalise the meta-critic into believing that genre has nothing to say about false readings. Genre remains a discriminator amongst readings—and if that is some solace in storms of criticism, so is the saw that we learn from our mistakes.

NOTES

1. Rosalie Colie, " 'All in Peeces': Problems of Interpretation in Donne's Anniversary Poems," in P. A. Fiore, ed., *Just So Much Honor: Essays Commemorating the Four-Hundreth Anniversary of the Birth of John Donne* (University Park: Pennsylvania State University Press, 1972), 214 and 189.

2. Rosalie Colie, *The Resources of Kind*, ed. Barbara K. Lewalski (Berkeley: University of California Press, 1973), 114–15.

3. Barbara L. Estrin, *Laura: Uncovering Gender and Genre in Wyatt, Donne and Marvell* (Durham, NC: Duke University Press, 1994).

4. Richard Halpern, "The Lyric in the Field of Information: Autopoiesis and History in Donne's Songs and Sonnets, in *Critical Essays on John Donne*, ed. A. F. Marotti (New York: G.K. Hall, 1994), 49–76.

5. Camille Wells Slights, "Participating Wisely in *Satyre III,*" *John Donne Journal* 10 (1991): 92.

6. Slights, "Participating Wisely," 93.

7. Slights, "Participating Wisely," 94.

8. Paul Sellin, "Satyre III No Satire: Postulates for Group Discussion," *John Donne Journal* 10 (1991): 85–89.

9. M. Thomas Hester, "Genre, Grammar, and Gender in Donne's Satyre III," *John Donne Journal* 10 (1991): 98.

10. Hester, "Genre, Grammar, and Gender," 98–99.

11. Hester, "Genre, Grammar, and Gender," 101.

12. Heather Dubrow, "Tradition and the Individualistic Talent" in *The Eagle and the Dove: Reassessing John Donne*, ed. (Columbia: University of Missouri Press, 1986); " 'The Sun in Water': Donne's Somerset Epithalamium and the Poetics of Patronage," in *The Historical Renaissance: New Essays on Tudor and Stuart Literature and Culture*, ed. H. Dubrow and R. Strier (Chicago: University of Chicago Press, 1988).

13. Dubrow, "Tradition and the Individualistic Talent," 115.

14. See, for example, John Carey, *John Donne: Life, Mind and Art* (London: Faber and Faber, 1983), 86–87.

15. Dubrow, "Tradition and the Individualistic Talent," 115.

16. Thomas O. Sloane, *Donne, Milton, and the End of Humanist Rhetoric* (Berkeley: University of California Press, 1985), 165.

17. John T. Shawcross, "Poetry, Personal and Impersonal: *The Case of Donne*," in Claude J. Summers and Ted-Larry Pebworth (eds.), *The Eagle and the Dove*, ed. Summers and Pebworth, 53–66.

Contributors

F. W. Brownlow is Gwen and Allen Smith Professor in English at Mount Holyoke College. His most recent book is *Robert Southwell* (1996).

A. D. Cousins is an Associate Professor of English at Macquarie University. He has been a Visiting Fellow at Princeton University, a Visiting Scholar at Penn State, and an Adjunct Professor at the Massachusetts Center for Renaissance Studies. He has written or edited several books on English Renaissance literature, most recently, *Shakespeare's Sonnets and Narrative Poems*.

Heather Dubrow, John Bascom Professor and Tighe-Evans Professor at the University of Wisconsin-Madison, is the author of five scholarly books, of which the most recent is *Shakespeare and Domestic Loss: Forms of Deprivations, Mourning, and Recuperation* (1999). Her other publications include a co-edited collection, numerous articles on early modern literature and pedagogy, and a chapbook of poetry; another chapbook is forthcoming.

Damian Grace teaches at the Faculty of Arts and Social Sciences at The University of New South Wales, and is currently Chair of Faculty. He teaches ethics and Renaissance philosophy to undergraduate students, and professional ethics to graduate students in his Faculty's postgraduate ethics programs. His principal research and writing are on the works of Thomas More and Tudor political theory, and on normative and applied ethics.

Eugene D. Hill is a Professor of English at Mount Holyoke College. He has published *Edward, Lord Herbert of Cherbury* (1987) and essays on Elizabethan tragedy. He coedited the forthcoming *Garland Encyclopedia of Tudor England*.

N. H. KEEBLE is a Professor and currently Head of the Department of English Studies at the University of Stirling, Scotland. His research interests are in English cultural history (and particularly literary and religious history) of the early modern period. His publications include studies and editions of Richard Baxter, John Bunyan, Lucy Hutchinson, Andrew Marvell, and John Milton. An edited contribution to the complete Yale edition of Marvell's prose, of which Annabel Patterson is general editor, and his *Cambridge Companion to Writing of the English Revolution* are forthcoming. He is currently at work on a study of the 1660s. Professor Keeble is a Fellow of the Royal Historical Society and of the English Association.

EARL MINER is Professor Emeritus of English and Comparative Literature at Princeton University. His interests are early modern British literature, classical Japanese literature, and comparative poetics.

MAREA MITCHELL lectures in Medieval and Renaissance studies at Macquarie University, and is particularly interested in feminism and cultural materialism. Her publications and current research include work on Beaumont and Fletcher's *Love's Cure, The Book of Margery Kempe*, and historical analysis on the genre of romance.

L. E. SEMLER teaches Medieval and Renaissance Literature at Macquarie University, Sydney, and the University of Newcastle, NSW. In 1997 he was Visiting Research Fellow at the Massachusetts Center for Renaissance Studies. He is author of numerous articles on seventeenth-century literature and *The English Mannerist Poets and the Visual Arts* (Fairleigh Dickinson University Press, 1998) and *Eliza's Babes; Or The Virgin's Offering (1652): A Critical Edition* (Fairleigh Dickinson University Press, 2000).

Index

Aretino, P., 44, 47
Aristotle, 127
Augustine, Saint, 87

Bakhtin, M., 9, 17
Bald, R., 116
Barclay, W., 127–28
Beaumont, W., 28
Bedford, Lady, 88–89
Bronzino, A., 44
Brooke, C., 42–43, 45
Browning, R., 82
Buchanan, G., 127
Buxton, J., 17

Calvin, J., 91, 123–24, 134
Campion, T., 72–73, 75
Capellanus, A., 13
Carew, T., 15, 34–35, 73–74
Catullus, 72
Charles I, 28, 125–26
Chaucer, G., 72
Cicero, 50, 53, 55
Colie, R., 9, 76, 138, 141, 143
Contarini, 125

Daniel, S., 76, 79
Donne, J., works of: "All haile sweet
  Poët," 47, 74; "The Anagram," 25, 27,
  48–49, 51, 59, 61–63, 68, 69; "The Anniversarie," 78; "The Anniversaries,"
  24, 37, 106–18, 138; "As due by many
  titles," 95; "The Autumnall," 59–62,
  68–69; "Batter my heart," 10, 15–16,
  34–35, 99; *Biathanatos*, 94; "The Blossome," 36, 80; "The Bracelet," 48, 50;
  "Breake of Day," 24; "The Calme," 42;
  "The Canonization," 78, 80; "Change,"
  48; "The Comparison," 48–50, 59, 62–
  67, 69; *Courtier's Library*, 94; "The

Curse," 59, 81; "Death be not proud,"
100; "The Dream," 79; "Epithalamion
made at Lincolnes Inne," 68; "An
Epithalamium at the Marriage of the
Earl of Somerset," 141–43; "An Epithalamium or Marriage Song on the Lady
Elizabeth," 141; "The Expiration," 74;
"The Extasie," 36, 80; "The Flea," 36;
"The Funerall," 121; "Goe, and catche
a falling starre," 25; "The good-
morrow," 80; "Goodfriday, 1613. Riding Westwood," 35–36; "His Picture,"
48–50; Holy Sonnets, 92–102;
"Hymne to God my God, in my sicknesse," 35; "A Hymne to God the
Father," 33–34; "If poysonous miner-
alls," 98; *Ignatius his Conclave*, 94; "The
Indifferent," 32; "Jealosie," 49; "La Corona," 89–92; "A Lecture upon the
Shadow," 80; "The Legacie," 82; letter
to Henry Goodyer, 76; letter to Lucy,
Countess of Bedford, 29–30; "Letter to
the Lady *Carey*, and Mrs *Essex Riche*,"
48; "Loves Alchymie," 74; "Loves
diet," 79; "Loves Warre," 48, 52;
"Marry, and love thy *Flavia*," 25; "The
Message," 59; "Nature's lay Ideot," 49,
51, 56; "Oh my blacke Soule!," 96; "On
his Mistris," 49, 52; "The Perfume,"
49, 67; "Pregnant again with th'old
twins Hope, and Fear," 47; "The Progresse of the Soul," 37; *Pseudomartyr*,
88; "Satyre I," 27, 59; "Satyre II," 26,
77; "Satyre III," 24, 139–41; "Satyre
IV," 26, 27, 78; "Sermon at St Paul's,
1630," 122; sermon of January 25,
1628, 121; sermon of January 25,
1629, 123–24; sermon of February 20,
1629, 128; "Show me deare Christ,"
24; "The Sunne Rising," 10–12, 32–33,